Smart Travel 18 National Parks in the Midwest & Eastern U.S.

Camping & Hiking Guide

(Also Mt. Rushmore National Memorial & Three 14-Day Park Hopper Travel Plans)

BY
Rob J. Simms

Copyright © 2019 – *CSBA Publishing House*

Email:csbapublishing@gmail.com

All Rights Reserved.

No part of this publication may be reproduced, stored in a retrieval system or transmitted in any form or by any means, electronic, mechanical, photocopying, recording or otherwise without the proper written consent of the copyright holder, except brief quotations used in a review.

Published by:

CSBA Publishing House

Cover & Interior designed

By

Denise Nicholson

First Edition

TABLE OF CONTENTS

Acknowledgements 6
Introduction 7
Part – 1 8
18 National Parks in the Midwest & Eastern United States 8
Guadalupe Mountains, Texas 9
Big Bend, Texas 13
Badlands, South Dakota 17
Mount Rushmore national Memorial, South Dakota 21
Wind Cave, South Dakota 24
Theodore Roosevelt, North Dakota 28
Voyageurs, Minnesota 32
Isle Royale, Michigan 36
Cuyahoga Valley, Ohio 40
Gateway Arch, Missouri 44
Hot Springs, Arkansas 47
Great Smoky Mountains, Tennessee, and North Carolina 50
Congaree, South Carolina 55
Mammoth Cave, Kentucky 58
Shenandoah, Virginia 62
Everglades, Florida 67
Dry Tortugas, Florida 71
Biscayne, Florida 75
Acadia, Maine 78
Part -2 82
What to See in a Day-Trip 82
Guadalupe Mountains, Texas 83
Big Bend, Texas 86
    Sam Nail Ranch 87
    Blue Creek Ranch Overlook 87
    Sotol Vista Overlook 87
    Lower Burro Mesa Pouroff 87
    Mule Ears Viewpoint 87
    Tuff Canyon 88
    Castolon Historic District 88
    Santa Elena Canyon 88
Badlands, South Dakota 89

Wind Cave, South Dakota ... 92
Theodore Roosevelt, North Dakota ... 94
- South Unit ... 94
- Elkhorn Ranch Unit ... 95
- North Unit ... 95

Hiking Options ... 95
- Easy Trails ... 96
- Moderate Trails ... 96
- Strenuous Trails ... 96

Voyageurs, Minnesota ... 97
Isle Royale, Michigan ... 99
Cuyahoga Valley, Ohio ... 101
Gateway Arch, Missouri ... 104
Hot Springs, Arkansas ... 106
Great Smoky Mountains, Tennessee, and North Carolina ... 109
Congaree, South Carolina ... 111
Mammoth Cave, Kentucky ... 113
Shenandoah, Virginia ... 115
Everglades, Florida ... 117
Dry Tortugas, Florida ... 119
Biscayne, Florida ... 121
Acadia, Maine ... 123

Part – 3 ... **126**
14-Day Park Hopper Travel Plans ... **126**
Two-Week Trip Itineraries ... 126

Itinerary #1: Texas ... 127
The Guadalupe Mountains and Big Bend ... 127
Guadalupe Mountains ... 127
- McKittrick Canyon ... 127
- Frijole Ranch ... 127
- Dog Canyon ... 128
- Williams Ranch ... 128
- Salt Basin Dunes ... 128

Big Bend ... 129
- Paved Scenic Drives ... 129
- Improved Dirt Scenic Drives ... 131
- Primitive Dirt Scenic Roads ... 132
- Desert Hikes ... 134

  Mountain Hikes 136
  River Hikes 138

Itinerary #2: South Dakota 140

 Badlands and Wind Cave 140
 Badlands 140
  Hiking Trails 141

 Wind Cave 142
  Cave Tours 142
  Garden of Eden Tour – Easy 142
  Natural Entrance Tour – Moderate 143
  Fairgrounds Tour – Strenuous 143

 Hiking Trails 144
  Easy Trails 144
  Moderate Trails 144
  Strenuous Trails 145

Itinerary #3: Florida 146

 Everglades, Dry Tortugas, and Biscayne 146
 Everglades 146
  Bicycling 146
  Birdwatching 146
  Boating 147
  Camping 147
  Kayaking and Canoeing 147
  Fishing 147

 Hiking 147
  Ranger Guided Programs 148
  Slough Slogging 149
  Tours 149
  Wildlife Viewing 149

 Dry Tortugas 149
  Garden Key 150
  Loggerhead Key 150
  Bush Key 151

 Biscayne 151
  Fishing 151
  Guided Tours 152

    Kayaking and Canoeing 152
    Diving and Snorkeling 152
    Boating 152
    Wildlife Watching 152
Last Word 153
A Final Note 156

ACKNOWLEDGMENTS

This work would not have been possible without the support of a few very special people. I want to especially thank my dear friend Jack Tillman for all his contribution, hard work, and dedication to this three book project.

I am also indebted to my brother Bobby Simms who inspired me to document my trips and start writing, who also has been supportive of my career goals and worked actively to provide me the support I needed to pursue my goals.

I am grateful to all those with whom I have had the pleasure to work with this and other related projects. Each member of my team has provided me extensive personal and professional guideline and taught me a great deal about both writing a book and publishing those works.

I would especially like to thank Denise Nicholson for her help and support in book layout, and design, without whom this monumental task would not have been done properly.

Nobody has been more important to me in the pursuit of this project than the members of my family. I would like to thank my parents, whose love and guidance are with me in whatever I pursue. They are the ultimate role models.

Most importantly, I wish to thank my loving and supportive wife Natalie, and my wonderful daughter, Liz, who always provides unending inspiration to everything I do. A special thanks to Wikipedia.org, Wikimedia.org and National Park Service for all the images and maps.

And….

To My Father, who taught me everything I know

To My Mother, without her, I won't be here

INTRODUCTION

Welcome to the third and final book in my three volume series all about our wonderful National Parks in our great, beautiful country. I hope you enjoyed reading my first two books "Smart Travel Guide to 16 National Parks in the Western United States" and "Smart Travel Guide to 13 National Parks in the Mountain West."

In this book, I am going to move on to the Mid-West and Eastern parts of the country. In this book, I will cover from the great state of Texas to the Dakotas, Michigan, Minnesota, Ohio, Missouri, Arkansas, Tennessee, and the Carolinas.

Similar to the other two guides, I'll give you a brief overview of what you need to know about each park. This is ideal for planning your trip, or for those who already know what they want to do at a National Park and just need to learn the basics before getting started.

The second part will give you some ideas for a day trip at each park. It is all about quick tours around historic areas, a hiking trail or two– the nutshell of what you should see at that particular location in the time you have there.

Then we'll give a couple of two-week itineraries if you want a longer vacation consisting of observing hidden wildlife creatures, exploring rich landscapes, going on more strenuous walks, and seeing the flora of each location in its peak blooming point.

So let's get started!

PART – 1

18 NATIONAL PARKS IN THE MIDWEST & EASTERN UNITED STATES

GUADALUPE MOUNTAINS, TEXAS

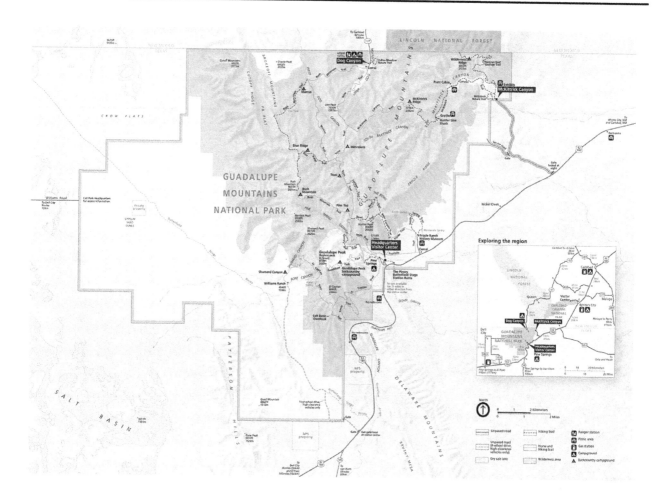

Overview

At the Guadalupe Mountains National Park you can visit one of the world's finest ancient fossilized Permian reefs, as well as the four highest peaks in Texas and a legally-designated wilderness full of unique flora and fauna. As promised, this area is rich in the local history of those who shaped the land. You can explore vast mountains, canyons, deserts, sand dunes, unlike any other National Park.

- **Visitor Centers / Hours**
    - The park is open year-round.

- Pine Springs Visitor Center is open every day except Christmas Day from 8 am to 4:30 pm.

- **Fees**
    - Admission fees are valid for seven days:
        - $5 per person over the age of 16.
    - There are additional fees for camping:
        - $8 per night per site.

- **Goods / Services**
    - There are no services in the park.

- **Pets**
    - Pets must be on a leash no longer than six feet and are only allowed in the following areas:
        - Roadsides
        - Parking areas
        - Picnic areas
        - Campgrounds

- **Camping**
    - Camping is available at two campgrounds.
        - Pine Springs Campground
            - 20 tent sites and 19 RV sites

- Campgrounds have potable water, flush toilets, utility sinks, and pay telephones. RV sites have no hook-ups, and there is no dump station.

☐ Dog Canyon Campground

- Nine tent sites and four RV sites

☐ **Reservations / Permits**

☐ Both campgrounds are available on a first come, first served basis.

☐ **Wildlife**

☐ Mule deer are most commonly seen near campgrounds or along park trails.
☐ Elk occasionally approaches springs or roadsides in the winter months.
☐ Other mammals that you may encounter include coyotes, gray foxes, desert cottontails, black-tailed jackrabbits, ringtails, and rock squirrels.
☐ Mountain lions, javelinas, and black bears are rarely seen in the park.
☐ Reptiles are seen in the warmer months, and you should be cautious for rattlesnakes.

☐ **Weather**

☐ Weather varies greatly throughout the year.
☐ Spring and summer feature warm and mild temperatures with the occasional rainfall.
☐ Fall and winter feature cooler temperatures and higher winds that can occasionally be higher than 70 mph.

- Snow and freezing fog can occur in the coldest months of December and January.

- **When to Visit**

    - Spring and summer tend to provide the best weather for visiting but arrive early to the desired campground if you wish to have a free spot.

- **Visiting Tips**

    - In addition to the two campsites, there are plenty of other backcountry campsites for those who want a more rural experience.
    - There are no available water sources in the backcountry, so bring plenty of water during your hikes.

BIG BEND, TEXAS

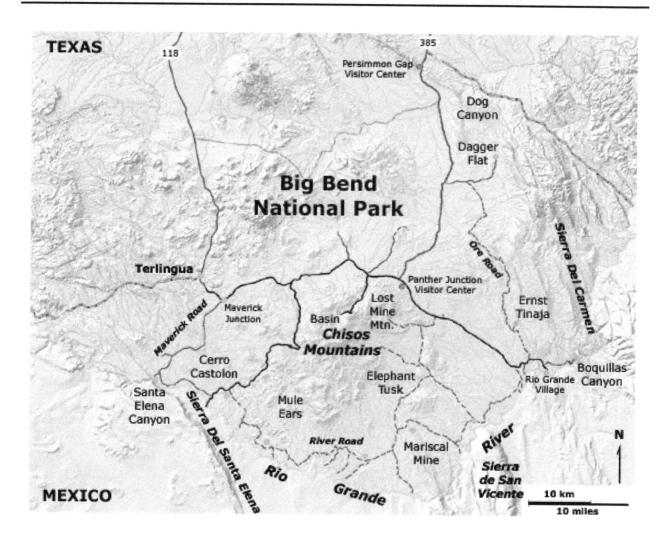

Overview

This unique National Park features geological structures dating back millions of years, along with 1,200 plant species and 450 bird species. Established as a National Park in 1935, Big Bend is an important preserve in southwest Texas. The entire park is 1,252 square miles, making it larger than the state of Rhode Island.

- **Visitor Centers / Hours**

    - The park is open year-round. There are five visitor centers, out of which three open seasonally.

- Chisos Basin, open daily 8:30 am to 4 pm.
- Panther Junction, open daily 8:30 am to 5 pm.
- Persimmon Gap, open November 1st to April 30th from 10 am to 4 pm.
- Castolon, open November 1st to April 30th from 10 am to 4 pm.
- Rio Grande Village, open November 1st to April 30th from 9 am to 4:30 pm.

Fees

- Admission fees are valid for seven days:
    - $30 per vehicle
    - $25 per motorcycle
    - $15 per individual
    - $55 for an annual pass

Goods / Services

- In addition to camping, you can stay at the Chisos Mountain Lodge if you prefer a more indoors-oriented setting.
- Convenience stores are available year-round at three locations:
    - Rio Grande Village
    - Chisos Basin
    - Castolon
- Limited groceries and gas can be found at two locations:
    - Panther Junction Service Station
    - Rio Grande Village Service Station
- Panther Junction also has a postal office open year-round.

- **Pets**
  - Pets must be on a leash no longer than six feet and are only allowed in the same areas where a car can go.

- **Camping**
  - Camping is available at three developed campgrounds with drinking water and restroom facilities:
    - Chisos Basin Campground, 60 sites, 26 reservable.
    - Cottonwood Campground, 24 sites, no reservations.
    - Rio Grande Village Campground, 100 sites, 43 reservable.

- **Reservations / Permits**
  - Two of three campgrounds have reservable campgrounds, and one is only available on a first come, first served basis.
  - Reservations can be made through recreation.gov up to six months in advance.

- **Wildlife**
  - The park is home to over 600 species of birds, mammals, reptiles, and amphibians.
  - Some of the most common you'll see are mule deer, ducks, geese, quail, coyotes, kangaroo rats, badgers (careful, as these are very temperamental), various bats and bobcats at nightfall, rabbits, and rattlesnakes.

- **Weather**
  - The park features numerous geographical regions so that the weather can vary greatly in each one. It is recommended to do

your research on the section you will visit beforehand in order to be prepared.
- Most of the area has mild winters, but snow and sub-freezing temperatures can happen at higher elevations.
- Summers tend to be hot and dry with low humidity. Afternoon thunderstorms may occur.

- **When to Visit**

    - The park can be visited year-round.
    - Spring and fall are the best times to visit when the days are mild and the nights are cool but not freezing.

- **Visiting Tips**

    - Wear a hat and sunglasses while dressing in layers. Expect a 20 degree (Fahrenheit) difference in temperature between low and high elevations.

BADLANDS, SOUTH DAKOTA

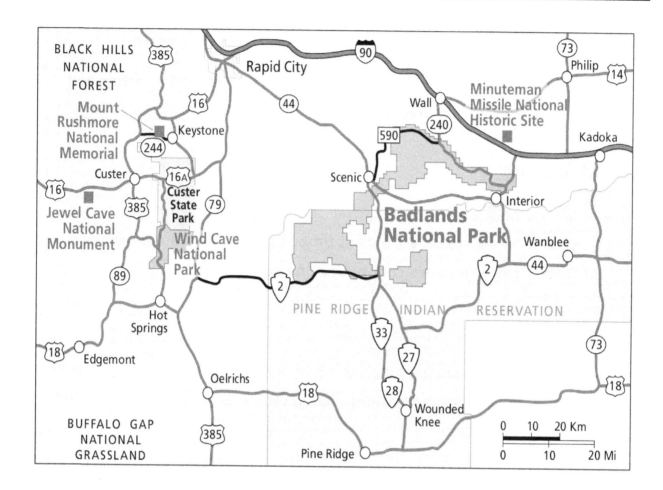

Overview

Badlands National Park is located along the end of the Great Plains in South Dakota. It consists of 244,000 acres of eroded buttes, pinnacles, and spires along with one of the largest protected prairies in the United States.

Badlands is well known for its fossil beds, allowing scientists to study the evolution of mammals like the horse, rhino, and saber-toothed cat. You'll also be able to view a wide range of wildlife species at this diverse and unique National Park.

☐ **Visitor Centers / Hours**

- The park is open year-round. There are two visitor centers, out of which one is open seasonally.

  - Ben Reifel Visitor Center

    - Open 8 am to 4 pm in the winter months.
    - Open 8 am to 5 pm in April and May.
    - Open 7 am to 7 pm in the summer months.
    - Open 8 am to 5 pm from early September to late October.

  - White River Visitor Center

    - Open 9 am to 5 pm in the summer months only.

- **Fees**
  - Admission fees are valid for seven days:

    - $20 per vehicle
    - $10 per motorcycle
    - $10 per individual
    - $40 for an annual pass

- **Goods / Services**

  - During the summer season, the Cedar Pass Lodge is open for lodging and a full-service restaurant.
  - No other services are offered in the park.

- **Pets**

- Pets must be on a leash no longer than six feet and are only allowed in the same areas where a car can go.

- **Camping**

    - Camping is available at two developed campgrounds that are open year-round.

        - Cedar Pass Campgrounds

            - 96 sites, reservable
            - $22 per night for two people, $4 per additional person
            - Cold water available and flushable toilets

        - Sage Creek Campground

            - No charge to camp
            - Pit toilets only and no ground fires allowed

- **Reservations / Permits**

    - Reservations need to be saved at the Cedar Pass Campgrounds and can be made through Forever Resorts at the website for the Cedar Pass Lodge.

- **Wildlife**
    - Portions of the park are set aside as restoration areas for the endangered black-footed ferret.
    - You can also expect to see porcupines, coyotes, bobcats, bison, bighorn sheep, and prairie dogs.

- **Weather**

    - The weather varies greatly throughout the year.

- Winters tend to be wet and cold while summers are hot and dry.
- Thunderstorms are likely to happen in the afternoons in summer.

- **When to Visit**

    - The park can be visited year-round, but avoid visiting in winter unless you have a specific craving for a few inches of snow and heavy blizzards.
    - Many choose to visit in August to view the Perseid meteor shower under clear skies.

- **Visiting Tips**

    - If hiking in the summer, drink plenty of water and reapply sunscreen frequently. There is little shade in the park and temperatures during the summer can easily get over 100 degrees Fahrenheit.
    - No matter what time of the year you visit, wear boots or closed-toe shoes due to cacti and rattlesnakes.
    - Watch your step, as the park is home to many burrowing animals and twisted ankles are a common injury.

MOUNT RUSHMORE NATIONAL MEMORIAL, SOUTH DAKOTA

Overview

Though Mount Rushmore is not a National Park, but it is well worth a trip to see the greatness of this national memorial which is only 85 miles East on I-90 from the Badlands National Park. This is where you get to see the true American History in all its glory. Majestic Figures of George Washington, Thomas Jefferson, Theodore Roosevelt and Abraham Lincoln, surrounded by the amazing landscape of the Black Hills of South Dakota.

- **Visitor Centers / Hours**

- The park is open year-round. The information center, visitor center, gift shop, and Carver's marketplace are open every day except December 25th.

    - Information & Visitor Centers

        - Open 8 am to 10 pm (Memorial Day to Mid-August).
        - Open 8 am to 9 pm (August 15th through September 30th).
        - Open 8 am to 5 pm (October 1st through Memorial Day)

- **Fees**

There are no fees to enter Mount Rushmore.
- $10 per vehicle parking fee
- $50 per commercial bus
- $25 per school bus

- **Walking/Hiking**

    - A short stroll along the Presidential Trail will provide close access to the sculpture.
    - More intimate views of the artwork are available along the way as either a self- guided or ranger-guided walk.
    - Two other trails lead to Borglum View Terrace and the Sculptor's Studio: One is a nature trail that starts from the main entryway; the other is a steep trail with uneven steps that starts from Grandview Terrace.

- **Nearby Activities**
    - Fishing

- ☐ Climbing
- ☐ Horseback Riding
- ☐ Mountain Biking
- ☐ Rockhounding
- ☐ Camping

☐ **Weather**

- ☐ The weather varies greatly throughout the year.
- ☐ May and June are the two wettest months of the year
- ☐ Winters tend to be wet and cold while summers are hot and dry.
- ☐ Thunderstorms are likely to happen in the afternoons in summer.

☐ **When to Visit**

- ☐ The park can be visited year-round, but avoid visiting in winter unless you have a specific craving for a few inches of snow and heavy blizzards.
- ☐ Many choose to visit in August to view the Perseid meteor shower under clear skies.

☐ **Visiting Tips**

- ☐ If hiking in the summer, drink plenty of water and reapply sunscreen frequently. There is little shade in the park and temperatures during the summer can easily get over 100 degrees Fahrenheit.

WIND CAVE, SOUTH DAKOTA

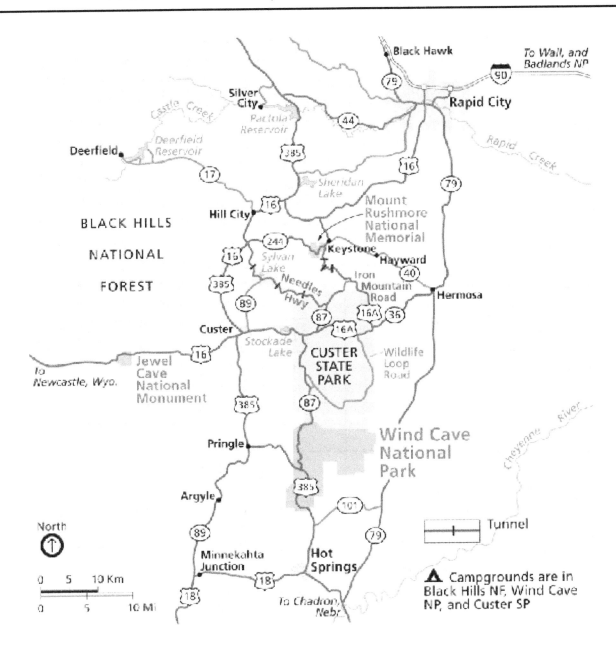

Overview

At Wind Cave National Park you can explore one of the longest and most complex caves in the world. Above ground, the park offers a mixed-grass prairie with plenty of wildlife viewing opportunities. The area was first discovered in 1881. This is truly a unique and wonderful park to visit.

- **Visitor Centers / Hours**

- The park is open year-round. However, some sections can have limited access in winter months. There is one visitor center.
- The Wind Cave Visitor Center is open year-round from 8 am to 4:30 pm except on Thanksgiving, Christmas, and New Year's Day.

- **Fees**

  - There are no fees to enter or hike through the park. Fees are collected for the cave tours and are as follows:

Age	Garden of Eden	Natural Entrance	Fairgrounds	Candlelight	Wild Cave
Adult (17+)	$10	$12	$12	$12	$30
Children (6-16)	$5	$6	$6	Ages 8+ $6	Not Permitted
Under 5	Free	Free	Free	Not Permitted	Not Permitted
Senior Access Pass	$5	$6	$6	$6	

  - Tickets are first come, first served and reservations are only for school groups or large groups.

- **Goods / Services**

  - There are no services in the park.

- **Pets**

  - Pets must be on a leash no longer than six feet and are only allowed in the following areas of the park:
    - Grassy areas near the Visitor Center
    - Elk Mountain Campground

- Prairie Vista Nature Trail
- Elk Mountain Nature Trail

- **Camping**
  - Camping is available at the Elk Mountain Campground. It costs $18 per night when water and toilet facilities are available. From later fall to early spring, the water is turned off, and the fee is $9 per night.

- **Reservations / Permits**
  - There is a self-registration area, and you should register upon arrival.

- **Wildlife**
  - The park is home to many native animal species such as bison, raccoons, skunks, elk, pronghorn, mule deer, coyotes, and prairie dogs. Beware of cougars and bobcats during nightfall in more seemingly isolated places.

- **Weather**
  - The area features weather extremes, and you should come prepared.
  - In the summer, severe thunderstorms are common with a potential for lightning and damaging hail.
  - Winter can bring harsh snow conditions.
  - Regardless of the temperatures and conditions above ground, the cave maintains a steady climate of about 50 degrees Fahrenheit.

- **When to Visit**

- The park can be visited year-round, but avoid visiting in winter unless you want severe weather with likely snowfall.
- Often, people prefer to visit in the spring when the weather is mild, and you have your best wildlife-viewing opportunities surrounded by blooming wildflowers.

- **Visiting Tips**

    - Taking a cave tour can be physically and mentally challenging. Consider avoiding the tour if you have claustrophobia issues.
    - If you plan to tour the caves, you should wear a light jacket and sturdy walking or hiking shoes.
    - Be prepared for spotty to no cell phone coverage.
    - Rattlesnakes are common throughout the park, so watch your footing.

THEODORE ROOSEVELT, NORTH DAKOTA

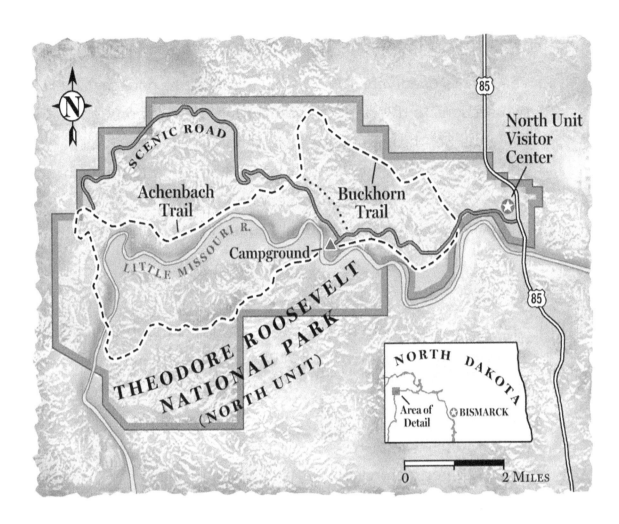

Overview

Theodore Roosevelt first traveled to the badlands area in 1883 while on a hunting trip. He was enchanted by the clean air, the endless meadows, and the freedom. It was here where he established a cattle business and first decided to find ways conserve land and wildlife.

As President of the United States, Roosevelt started the US Forest Service as well as the 1906 Antiquities Act that established 18 national monuments, five national parks, 51 wildlife refuges, and 150 national forests. Today, Theodore

Roosevelt National Park offers a colorful place to enjoy an astounding quantity of plants and animals.

- **Visitor Centers / Hours**
    - The park is open year-round. It is important to note that there are two sections to this park: the North Unit operates on Central Time, while the South Unit operates on Mountain Time.
    - The South Unit Visitor Center is open 8 am to 4:30 pm with extended hours June through September.
    - The Painted Canyon Visitor Center doesn't open until May.

- **Fees**
    - Fees are collected at entrance stations May through September and at visitor centers the rest of the year. Fees are valid for seven days.
        - $30 per vehicle
        - $25 per motorcycle
        - $15 per individual
        - $55 for an annual pass

- **Goods / Services**
    - There are no services in the park.

- **Pets**
    - Pets must be on a leash no longer than six feet and are only allowed in the following areas of the park:
        - Roads and road shoulders
        - Sidewalks

- Parking areas
- Campgrounds
- Picnic areas

- **Camping**
    - Camping is available at two campgrounds: Juniper Campground in the North Unit and Cottonwood Campground in the South Unit.
    - All of the sites in the Juniper Campground and half the side in the Cottonwood Campground are first come, first served.
    - Winter rates are $7 per night. Summer rate is $14 per night.

- **Reservations / Permits**
    - Half the sites at the Cottonwood Campground can be reserved through recreation.gov.

- **Wildlife**
    - There is a variety of animals to see at this park, although what you see will depend on the season you visit.
    - Some of the animals you may catch a glimpse of include bison, mule deer, white-tailed deer, elk, feral horses, longhorns, pronghorns, coyotes, bobcats, badgers, beavers, porcupines, prairie dogs, and golden eagles.

- **Weather**
    - Summers tend to be warm with average temperatures of 70 to 80 degrees Fahrenheit.
    - Winters are cold, sporting average temperatures in the single digits.
    - Wind is considerably strong year-round.
    - Rain is infrequent but brings large amounts once it pours down.

- Snow is common in the winter months.

- **When to Visit**

    - Summer tends to be the best time to visit the park.

- **Visiting Tips**

    - A must-visit site is the Cannonball Concretions Pull Out in the North Unit of the park.

VOYAGEURS, MINNESOTA

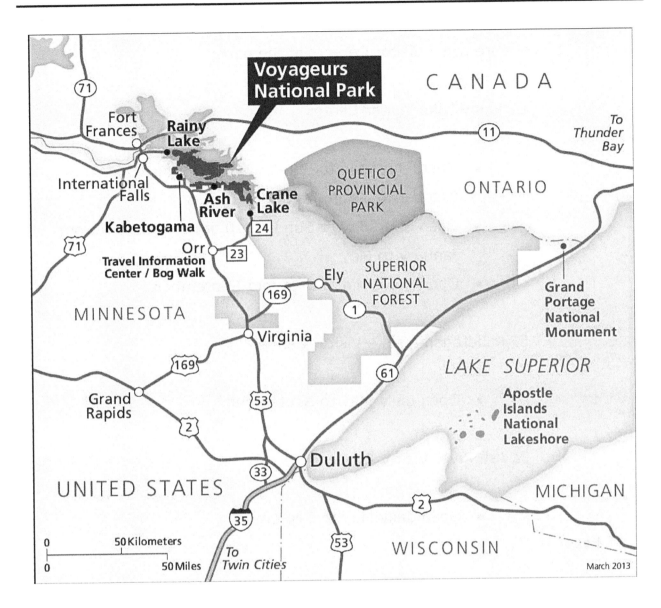

Overview

When you visit the Voyageurs National Park, you will see a number of waterways that flow into the Hudson Bay. The area is home to several aquatic and forest ecosystems. In order to fully experience this park, you'll want to get out of your vehicle and head out into the water, or at least explore the shorelines.

- **Visitor Centers / Hours**

- The park is open year-round. However, in the winter months, you'll need to be prepared for snowy conditions.
- There are three Visitor Centers in the park:

  - Rainy Lake Visitor Center

    - Open Thursday to Sunday, 10 am to 4 pm from October to December.
    - Open Thursday to Sunday, 10 am to 4:30 pm from January to May
    - Open daily mid-May to mid-September.

  - Kabetogama Lake Visitor Center

    - Open daily May to September

  - Ash River Visitor Center

    - Open daily May to September

- **Fees**

  - There is no fee to enter the park.
  - There are fees for camping and boat rentals, so contact the park for details as the fees vary by site, location and time of your visit.

- **Goods / Services**

  - Within the park, Kettle Falls Hotel offers lodging and dining options during certain times of the year.

- **Pets**

- Pets must be on a leash no longer than six feet and are only allowed in the following areas of the park:
    - Within campsites
    - Along the Recreation Trail
    - Visitor center areas
    - Parking lots

- **Camping**
    - It is important to note that all campsites are only accessible by watercraft.
    - There are over 270 sites available as tent campsites, houseboat sites, and day use sites.

- **Reservations / Permits**
    - You can make reservations through recreation.gov.

- **Wildlife**
    - The most common animals you'll encounter in the park are various types of waterfowl, moose, beaver, wolves, bald eagles, common loons, and double-crested cormorants.

- **Weather**
    - There are four distinct seasons in the park.
    - The most temperate times are June, July, and August.
    - Snowfall typically starts in late October and continues until about late April or early May.
    - Frost-free days are typically from June to mid-September.

- **When to Visit**
    - June, July, and August are the most popular times for visitors.

- **Visiting Tips**
    - Be sure to follow boating guides, as there are many potential hazards and harsh currents.
    - Visit in the winter months to see the beautiful aurora borealis known as the "Northern Lights," as well as shooting stars, meteors, and gazing in marvel at the Milky Way as it spreads before your eyes.

ISLE ROYALE, MICHIGAN

Overview

Located in Lake Superior off the short of Michigan, you'll find the 850 square mile Isle Royale National Park. The park is characterized by crystal waters and rugged shorelines. It was created from ancient lava flows. You can hike among 165 miles of scenic trails or stay at one of 36 campgrounds. You can also tour historic lighthouses, shipwrecks, and copper mines. This national park is only accessible by boat or float plane.

- **Visitor Centers / Hours**

    - The park is open from April 16th to October 31st. It is closed from November 1st to April 15th due to extreme winter weather.
    - There are two visitor centers on the island and one in nearby Houghton, Michigan.

- Houghton Visitor Center in Houghton, Michigan.

  - June 1st to September 15th, open 8 am to 6 pm Monday to Friday, and 10 am to 6 pm on Saturday.
  - September 16th to May 31st, open 10 am to 4 pm Monday to Friday.

- Rock Harbor Visitor Center at the northeast end of the island.

  - Open July and August from 8 am to 6 pm daily.
  - Contact the park for reduced hours in May, June, and September.

- Windigo Visitor Center at the southwest end of the island

  - Open July and August from 8 am to 6 pm daily.
  - Contact the park for reduced hours in May, June, September, and October.

- **Fees**

  - The fee is $7 per day for people entering the park. Children under 15 are free.
  - A season pass is $60.

- **Goods / Services**

  - There are no services in the park.

- **Pets**

  - Pets are not allowed on the island or boats in the surrounding waters.

- **Camping**
  - There are 36 campgrounds located across the island.
  - All sites are available by foot or watercraft only.
  - Permits are required for overnight stays in boats, but campsites are first come, first served.

- **Reservations / Permits**
  - Contact the park for permits.

- **Wildlife**
  - The largest mammals seen on the island are moose and wolves.
  - The rest of the common animals seen are birds and amphibians.

- **Weather**
  - The harsh winter conditions make this park inaccessible in the winter.
  - The times when the park is open are great times to visit for water activities, as the weather is mild and warm.

- **When to Visit**
  - Any time the park is open is a great time to visit.

- **Visiting Tips**
  - For large groups, you should book travel well in advance due to limited seats on ferry boats.
  - Even in summer, the water is frigid and the evenings are cool so be sure to pack long sleeve clothing and wear layers.

- ☐ Access to services is limited, so pack extras of any necessary items.
- ☐ Mosquito repellent is recommended, as you would be close to a source of water.

CUYAHOGA VALLEY, OHIO

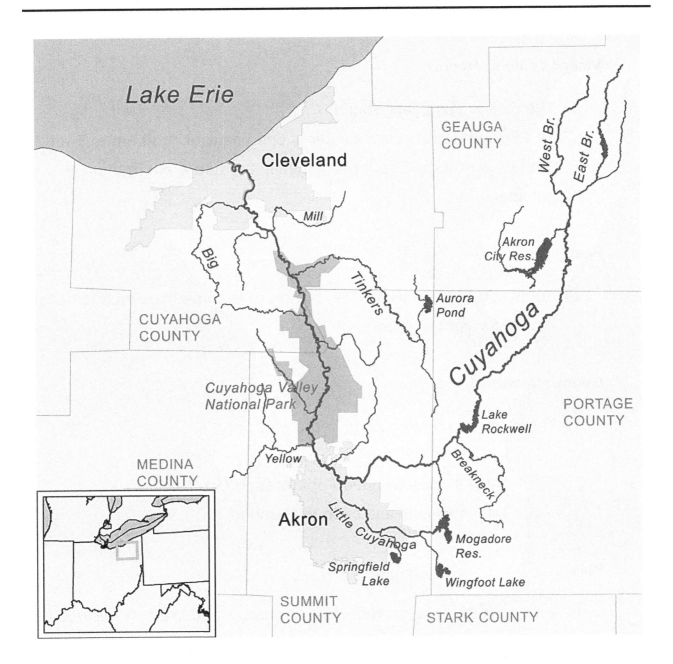

Overview

Cuyahoga means the "Crooked River," which also includes over 33,000 acres of forests, hills, and farmlands. This National Park is a great place to participate in recreational activities as well as enjoying a quiet sense of solitude. It was first created as a National Recreation Area in 1974, and later became a National Park in 2000. Here you can partake in outdoor activities including hiking, golfing, train rides, and kayaking in the warmer weather and snowshoeing or cross-country skiing in the winter months.

- **Visitor Centers / Hours**
    - The park is open year-round.
    - The Boston Store Visitor Center is open daily at 9:30 am to 5 pm in the fall, winter, and spring, then daily 8 am to 6 pm in the summer.

- **Fees**
    - Admission to the park is free, but there is sometimes an additional charge for special events.

- **Goods / Services**
    - There are two retail outlets in the park:
        - Trail Mix Boston open April through October
        - Trail Mix Peninsula open year-round

- **Pets**
    - Pets must be on a leash six feet or shorter and are only allowed at the following locations:
        - In the campground
        - On 110 miles of hiking trails

- **Camping**
    - There are only five primitive campsites in the park.
    - They are available from May 1st to October 31st.

- ☐ Reservations are required.
- ☐ Cost is $25 per night, plus a $3.50 reservation fee.

- ☐ **Reservations / Permits**
  - ☐ Reservations can be made through reserveamerica.com.

- ☐ **Wildlife**
  - ☐ The National Park land has been restored as a wildlife refuge. As a result, you will be able to see endangered species such as the bald eagle and peregrine falcons, among others.

- ☐ **Weather**
  - ☐ There are four seasons at this park.
  - ☐ Spring and fall offer pleasant and mild weather.
  - ☐ Summers are often hot, while winters are typically frigid.

- ☐ **When to Visit**
  - ☐ For the best weather, visit during spring and fall.

- ☐ **Visiting Tips**
  - ☐ It is recommended to hike earlier in the day rather than later, and if you plan to stay out longer, bring a flashlight and be mindful of trail hazards.
  - ☐ When hiking to the Ledges Overlook, stay back from the ledge and be careful, as the footing is dangerous.
  - ☐ Ticks are common in the park, so wear long pants and tuck them into socks or closed-toe shoes. Wearing light-colored clothing will also make the ticks easier to spot.

☐ Despite the snow, this National Park is still an excellent place to visit in the winter with the proper precautions and equipment in mind.

GATEWAY ARCH, MISSOURI

Overview

The main focus of this National Park is the Gateway Arch National Monument that was known as the Jefferson National Expansion Memorial until 2018. In addition to the Gateway Arch, the park is also home to the Museum of Westward Expansion and St. Louis' Old Courthouse.

Construction on the Arch began in 1963 and was completed in 1965 for less than $15 million. It is designed to withstand both earthquakes and high winds. Near the Arch is the Old Courthouse, which is one of the oldest buildings in St. Louis, dating back to 1839.

- **Visitor Centers / Hours**
    - The park is open year-round, except Thanksgiving, Christmas, and New Year's Day.

- The Gateway Arch is open daily 8 am to 10 pm in the summer, and daily 9 am to 6 pm in the winter.
- The park grounds are open daily from 5 am to 11 pm year-round.
- The Old Courthouse is open daily from 8 am to 4:30 pm year-round.

- **Fees**
  - The entrance fee to the park is $3 for anyone 16 and older.
  - There are additional fees for the tram ride to the top of the arch, the riverfront cruise, and to watch a movie about the arch.
- **Goods / Services**
  - There are two main retail outlets:
    - The Arch Store
    - The Old Courthouse Shop
  - Food is available at two concession stands:
    - The Arch Cafe
    - Arch View Café

- **Pets**
  - Only service pets are allowed.

- **Camping**
  - There is no camping, but the surrounding area provides plenty of lodging opportunities.
- **Reservations / Permits**

- ☐ You can contact the park in advance to purchase tour tickets or purchase them on the day of your trip.

☐ **Wildlife**

- ☐ You can expect to see turtles, snakes, the occasional crane, and waterfowl.

☐ **Weather**

- ☐ The park boasts of comfortable weather year-round. Cold winter weather is rare, with the lowest being about 32 degrees Fahrenheit.
- ☐ Summer is peak visit time, so be prepared for long lines and large crowds.

☐ **When to Visit**

- ☐ Perhaps the best time to visit is spring, as the weather is mild and the crowds are smaller.

☐ **Visiting Tips**

- ☐ Take the time to enjoy the vibrant downtown section of St. Louis during your stay.
- ☐ Be aware you'll need to pass through airport-style security when visiting the Arch.

HOT SPRINGS, ARKANSAS

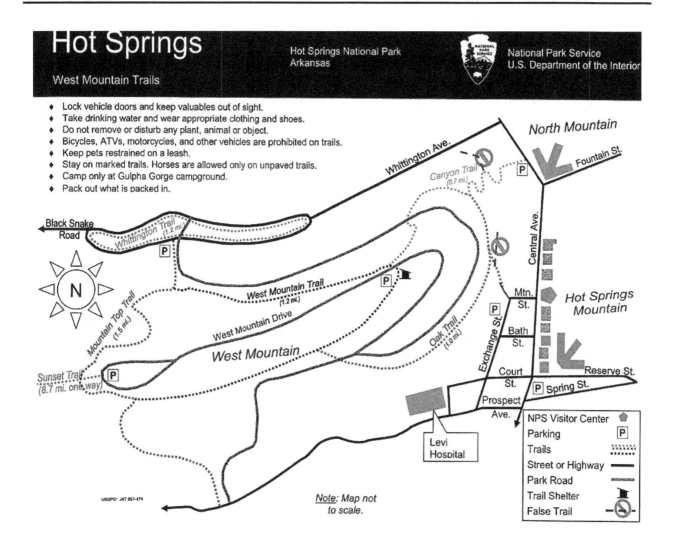

Overview

This popular National Park features 40 hot springs where you can go to relax and heal. It was originally established as the Hot Spring Reservation by Congress in 1832 and became a National Park in 1921.

Today, it is one of the oldest protected areas within the National Park system. In addition to the hot springs, you can explore 20 miles of wilderness trail areas or tour historic landscapes.

☐ **Visitor Centers / Hours**

- ☐ The park is open year-round.
- ☐ Fordyce Bathhouse Visitor Center is open daily 9 am to 5 pm.

☐ **Fees**

- ☐ There is no fee to enter the park.

☐ **Goods / Services**

- ☐ The park has a gift shop and bookstore.

☐ **Pets**

- ☐ Pets are welcome in the park but must stay outside park buildings.

☐ **Camping**

- ☐ Camping is available at Gulpha Gorge Campground.
- ☐ Camping is $30 per night, and all sites are first come, first served.

☐ **Reservations / Permits**

- ☐ There is no need for reservations.

☐ **Wildlife**

- ☐ You are most likely to encounter small mammals, rodents, and birds.
- ☐ Since this destination has a stable and warm climate, birds species are varied and plentiful.

☐ **Weather**

- ☐ Summers are hot and humid.
- ☐ Winter feels colder due to wind chill.

- **When to Visit**
    - Spring and fall are ideal times to visit when the weather is the mildest.

- **Visiting Tips**
    - Be sure to bring an empty jug so you can take home some free thermal water.
    - Be alert for snakes, since the area is home to copperheads, cottonmouths, and rattlesnakes.

GREAT SMOKY MOUNTAINS, TENNESSEE, AND NORTH CAROLINA

Overview

According to the National Geographic "Great Smoky Mountains National Park drew more than eleven million visitors last year—about twice the number of the second most popular park. Most visitors see the park from a mountain-skimming scenic highway; many take to the more than 800 miles of hiking trails across North Carolina and Tennessee." Out of the 59 parks, this is by far the most popular park in our great country.

Great Smoky Mountains National Park sits on the border between Tennessee and North Carolina. This place is known as the Smokies due to the heavy coat of morning fog that is always present.

The area is also famous for the wide array of plant and animal life, and the history of the Appalachian culture. There are over 80 historic buildings to see in this park and dozens of outdoor activities to enjoy.

- **Visitor Centers / Hours**
    - The park is open year-round. Although some secondary roads, campgrounds, and visitor facilities close during the winter months.
    - There are four visitor centers within the park:
        - Cades Cove Visitor Center is open every day except Christmas Day.
            - Hours vary from 9 am to 7 pm depending on the time of the year.
        - Oconaluftee Visitor Center is open every day except Christmas Day.
            - Hours vary from 8 am to 7 pm depending on the time of the year.
        - Sugarlands Visitor Center is open every day except Christmas Day.
            - Hours vary from 8 am to 7 pm depending on the time of the year.

- Clingmans Dome Visitor Center is open every day except Christmas Day.

    - Hours vary from 9:30 am to 6 pm depending on the time of the year.

- **Fees**

    - There is no fee to enter the park.

- **Goods / Services**

    - There are limited food and beverage services in the park at the following locations:

        - Cades Cove Campground Store
        - Elkmont Campground Concession
        - Cades Cove Visitor Center

- **Pets**

    - Dogs must be kept on a leash no more than six feet at all times. Dogs are allowed in the following areas:

        - Campgrounds
        - Picnic sections
        - Alongside the roads

- **Camping**

    - Several types of camping are available including frontcountry, backcountry, group, and horse camping.

- Developed campsites are found at 10 locations within the park:
    - Abrams Creek
    - Balsam Mountain
    - Big Creek
    - Cades Cove
    - Cataloochee
    - Cosby
    - Deep Creek
    - Elkmont
    - Look Rock
    - Smokemont

- Camping is $14-23 per night.

- **Reservations / Permits**

    - Some campsites can be reserved through recreation.gov.

- **Wildlife**

    - Over 17,000 species are known to live within the National Park.
    - The area is a common place to spot black bears, so be extremely careful during key seasons and avoid delving too deep into unmarked territories.

- **Weather**
    - March has the widest temperature range with snowfall possible at any time throughout the month.
    - Higher elevations can vary by 10 to 20 degrees Fahrenheit.
    - Afternoon showers and thunderstorms are possible in the summer.
    - Come prepared for any type of climate when visiting this park.

- **When to Visit**
    - Autumn is a wonderful time to visit since there are warm days and cool nights along with dry conditions.

- **Visiting Tips**
    - With so much to see or do at this park, be sure to plan an extended stay; you'll definitely want to come back again.

CONGAREE, SOUTH CAROLINA

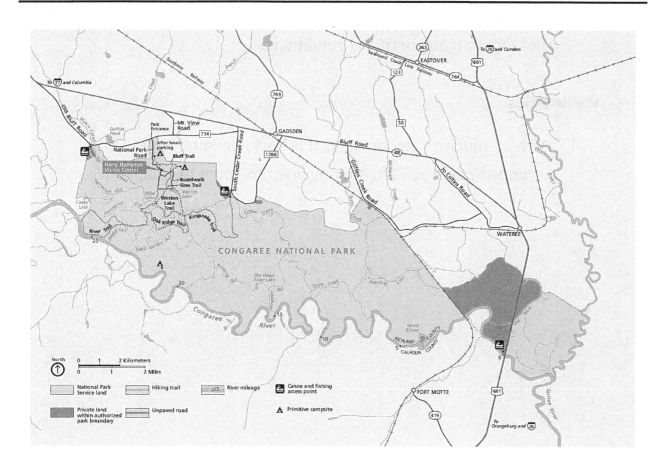

Overview

The Congaree National Park is home to some of the tallest trees in the eastern United States. Located in central South Carolina along the Congaree River, this 22,200-acre park protects a large old-growth hardwood forest as well as diverse plant and animal life. In fact, the floodplain of this forest has one of the highest canopies in the world. Take your time to walk around and relax in this wonderful wilderness space.

- **Visitor Centers / Hours**

    - The park is open year-round.
    - Harry Hampton Visitor Center is open daily from 9 am to 5 pm except on federal holidays.

- **Fees**
    - There is no fee to enter the park.

- **Goods / Services**
    - There are no goods or services available in the park, but rather in the surrounding areas.

- **Pets**
    - Pets are allowed in all areas of the park but must be on a leash no longer than six feet.

- **Camping**
    - Camping is available at one of two campgrounds:
        - Longleaf Campground is $10 per night for a tent site and $20 per night for a group site. There are 10 individual sites and four group sites available, all of which need to be reserved beforehand. There is no running water and only vault toilets.
        - Bluff Campground is $5 per night for a tent site. There are six sites and no vehicle access. There are also no restroom facilities or running water.

- **Reservations / Permits**
    - Campsites can be reserved through recreation.gov.

- **Wildlife**
    - The unique biosphere of the area makes it home to thousands of mammals, amphibians, reptiles, birds, and fish.

- **Weather**
    - The area has a generally humid subtropical climate. This means mild winters and summers that are very warm and wet.
    - June to August are the hottest times of the year.

- **When to Visit**
    - Spring and fall, or March to May, are the best times to visit when the weather is the mildest, and the insect activity is lowest.

- **Visiting Tips**
    - Be careful around downed trees, as this is where you'll find spiders, wasps, and snakes. The area is home to three venomous snakes including the water moccasin, the copperhead, and the rattlesnake.

MAMMOTH CAVE, KENTUCKY

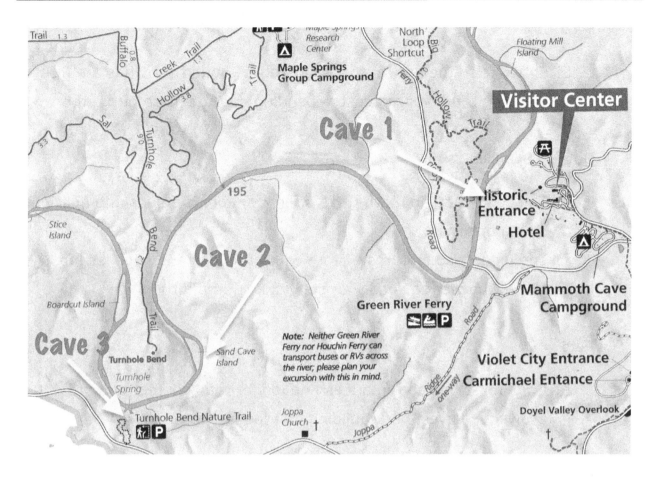

Overview

The main focus of the National Park is the preservation of a cave system below ground with the Green River Valley and rolling hills above ground. There are 10 miles of cave tunnels available for tours, but you can also do various outdoor activities above ground as well.

The National Park was formed in 1926 by a group of private citizens and was given its official title and standing in 1941. It was then declared a World Heritage Site in 1981 and later an International Biosphere Reserve in 1990.

- **Visitor Centers / Hours**
    - The park is open year-round.

- The Visitor Center is open daily 8:30 am to 4:30 pm.

- **Fees**

    - Entrance to the park is free, and above ground activities are free, but cave tours vary in cost depending on the length of the tour.

- **Goods / Services**

    - The Lodge at Mammoth Cave offers comfortable beds and delicious dining options.
    - The lodge also features a store with groceries and supplies for those who want a sugary or salty snack during their trip.

- **Pets**

    - Dogs must be kept on a leash no longer than six feet and are not allowed in caves, park buildings, or lodging facilities.

- **Camping**

    - Camping is available at three developed campgrounds and backcountry campsites.
        - Mammoth Cave Campground has 105 sites and is open seasonally by reservation.
            - $20 tent site, $25 group site, $50 RV site
        - Maple Springs Group Campground
            - $25 to $35 per campsite depending on hookups
        - Houchin Ferry Campground has 12 primitive campsites available year-round.
            - $15 per site

- **Reservations / Permits**

- Campsites can be reserved through recreation.gov.

- **Wildlife**

    - In the caves, you may spot occasional bats although they are on the decline due to the commotion of tours.
    - Above ground, you'll potentially spot black bears, white-tailed deer and a wide variety of birds.

- **Weather**

    - Summers are hot and dry.
    - Spring is cool and temperate.
    - Winters can vary greatly from regular cold winds to blizzard conditions.
    - However, the caves always maintain a steady temperature of 54 degrees Fahrenheit.

- **When to Visit**

    - If you are only visiting the cave, nearly any time of the year is appropriate to visit.
    - For above ground activities, you should come in the spring when the weather is more temperate.

- **Visiting Tips**

    - Make your reservations as quickly as possible since popular tours can be booked up to several months in advance, especially in summer and holiday weekends.
    - Plan at least two hours to tour the Visitor Center.

- In order to cross the Green River that divides the park you need to use one of two ferries; be patient, as sometimes there can be a long wait time.
- Flash photography, strollers, tripods, backpacks, and child carriers are not allowed in the caves.
- Ticks and chiggers are common insects in the area; it is also home to two poisonous snakes: the rattlesnake and the copperhead.

SHENANDOAH, VIRGINIA

Overview

If you are into 80's music, you may remember John Denver, his evergreen music and his love for the Blue Ridge Mountain and Shenandoah River. Every time I visit this park, I always listen to his music and always discover a different beauty of this region.

Shenandoah National Park sits beside the beautiful Blue Ridge Mountains in Virginia. You can see all the beauty of the park from the 105-mile drive along

Skyline Drive with 75 overlooks. Alternatively, you could take the initiative and hike one of 500 miles of trails that contain 101 miles of the Appalachian Trail.

There are plenty of recreational activities in this park that deserve multiple visits. This is perhaps the best outdoor experience you can have of any National Park.

- **Visitor Centers / Hours**
    - The park is open year-round. However, Skyline Drive may be closed due to inclement weather during certain winter months.
    - There are two visitor centers:
        - Dickey Ridge Visitor Center, open April 6th to November 25th daily from 9 am to 5 pm.
        - Byrd Visitor Center, open March 23rd to November 25th daily from 9 am to 5 pm.

- **Fees**
    - Entrance fees are valid for seven days:
        - $30 per vehicle
        - $25 per motorcycle
        - $15 per individual
        - $55 for an annual pass

- **Goods / Services**
    - Groceries, wood, ice, and camping supplies are available at the following locations:
        - Elkwallow Wayside

- ☐ Big Meadows Wayside
- ☐ Lewis Mountain Camp Store
- ☐ Loft Mountain Camp Store

☐ Big Meadows Wayside also has gas services.
☐ In addition to camping, lodging is available at the following locations:

- ☐ Big Meadows Lodge
- ☐ Skyland Resort
- ☐ Lewis Mountain Cabins

☐ Reservations can be made at GoShenandoah.com.
☐ Most lodges and a few stores have dining options as well.

☐ **Pets**

☐ Dogs must be on a leash no longer than six feet and are allowed on most trails except the following:

- ☐ Fox Hollow Trail
- ☐ Stony Man Trail
- ☐ Limberlost Trail
- ☐ Post Office Junction to Old Rag Shelter
- ☐ Old Rag Ridge Trail
- ☐ Old Rag Saddle Trail
- ☐ Dark Hollow Falls Trail
- ☐ The story of the Forest Trail
- ☐ Bearfence Mountain Trail
- ☐ Frazier Discovery Trail

- **Camping**
    - Camping is available at five developed campsites and many backcountry camping areas.
        - Matthew Arms Campground, $15
        - Big Meadows Campground, $20
        - Lewis Mountain Campground, $15
        - Loft Mountain Campground, $15
        - Dundo Group Campground varies
    - Most campgrounds feature hookups and amenities.

- **Reservations / Permits**
    - Campsites can be reserved through recreation.gov.

- **Wildlife**
    - The park is a refuge for many mammals including deer, black bears, and wild turkeys.
    - There is also a wide variety of insects and amphibians.

- **Weather**
    - Winters are typically cold and often have snow.
    - Summer can be balmy, with mountain elevations up to 10 degrees cooler along with fresh breezes.

- **When to Visit**
    - Spring and fall can bring in the mildest weather, but come prepared as you may likely experience all four seasons in a single day depending on the sections of the park you choose to explore.

- **Visiting Tips**
    - If hiking in warmer weather, plan to reach the peak of your climb by mid-afternoon.

EVERGLADES, FLORIDA

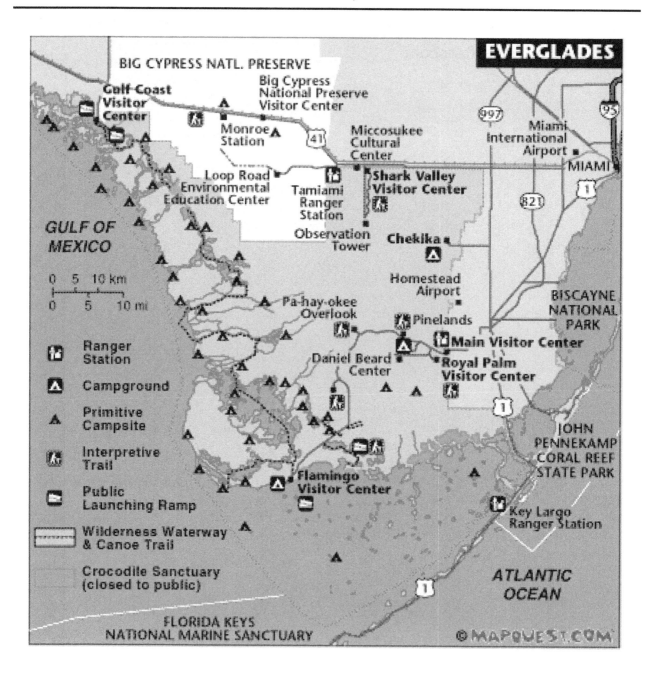

Overview

Everglades National Park is a large area of 1.5 million acres. It is a tropical and subtropical habitat with one of the most diverse ecosystems in the world. Everglades was established as a National Park by Congress in 1934. Since then, it has been named an International Biosphere Reserve, a Wetland of International Importance, and a World Heritage Site.

- **Visitor Centers / Hours**
    - The park is open year-round.
    - There are four visitor centers:
        - Ernest F. Coe Visitor Center. Open daily 9 am to 5 pm.
        - Shark Valley Visitor Center. Open daily 9 am to 5 pm.
            - Offers nearby tram tours of the area.
        - Gulf Coast Visitor Center. Open daily 9 am to 4:30 pm.
            - Boat tours are available from this area.
        - Flamingo Visitor Center. Open intermittently from 8 am to 4:30 pm based on staffing.

- **Fees**
    - Entrance fees are valid for seven days:
        - $25 per vehicle
        - $20 per motorcycle
        - $8 per individual
        - $40 for an annual pass

- **Goods / Services**
    - There are no goods and services in the park.

- **Pets**

- Pets are allowed on a leash no longer than six feet and only in the following areas:

  - Roadways open to public traffic
  - Campgrounds
  - Picnic areas
  - Maintained grounds around public facilities and residential locations
  - Private boats

- **Camping**

  - Camping is available at two developed campgrounds and backcountry camping:

    - Long Pine Key Campground. Open November 1st to April 30th. 108 tent spaces and RV sites available as first come, first served for $20 per night.
    - Flamingo Campground. Open year-round, reservations needed from November 20th to April 15th. There are 234 sites with prices standing at $20 per night with no hookups, and 41 sites with electric hookups at $30 per night.

- **Reservations / Permits**

  - Reservations need to be made through Everglades Guest Services.

- **Wildlife**

  - The area features five different habitats: the Hammock, Mangrove, Pineland, Sawgrass, and Slough.
  - The most common animal you'll see is the alligator and Burmese Python

- Other animals in the area include manatees, white-tailed deer, bobcats, and several endangered animals such as the crocodile and the Florida panther.

- **Weather**
  - The tropical environment means there are just two seasons: wet and dry.
  - The dry season is from December to April. This is when the humidity is low, and temperatures are typically between 53 to 77 degrees Fahrenheit.
  - The wet season is from May to November. Humidity rises and rain is common for this very reason, with heated temperatures of often over 90 degrees Fahrenheit.

- **When to Visit**
  - Most people choose to visit during the dry season since the weather is more favorable and the water levels are lower, making it easier to view wildlife.

- **Visiting Tips**
  - If you plan to hike in the backcountry, beware of dangers such as alligators, cottonmouth snakes, poison ivy, poisonwood sprinkle rock pinelands, and the manchineel. Avoid approaching the water in general unless you make sure there are no temperamental reptiles.
  - Drive slowly on the Main Park Road and the Tamiami Trail in order to avoid hitting critters such as turtles, snakes, and sometimes the endangered Florida panther.

DRY TORTUGAS, FLORIDA

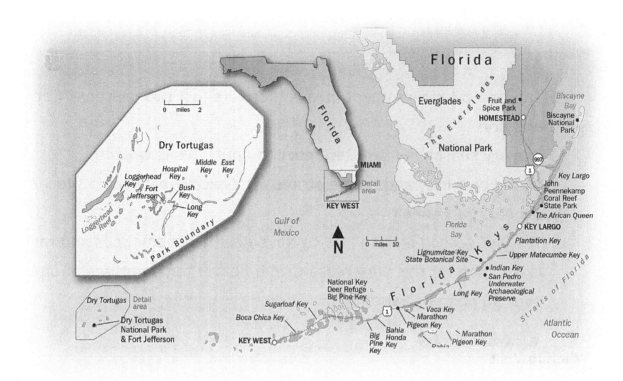

Overview

Located near Key West, Florida, Dry Tortugas is an excellent beach vacation where you can bird-watch and snorkel alongside colorful fish. Dry Tortugas National Park is made up of seven islands and the waters surrounding them. The main attraction here is Fort Jefferson built from 1846 to 1875.

While never finished, it is one of the largest masonry structures in the Western Hemisphere. It is also one of the most remote parks in the National Park System, and you can only access it by ferry, seaplane, private boat, or charter boat.

- **Visitor Centers / Hours**

- The park is open year-round although some islands are closed to the public.

  - Garden Key is open year-round 24 hours a day.
  - Fort Jefferson on Garden Key is open year-round from sunrise to sunset.
  - Loggerhead Key is open year-round from sunrise to sunset.
  - Bush Key is closed seasonally for sooty tern nesting season. It is typically open from mid-October to mid-January.
  - East Key, Middle Key, Hospital Key, and Long Key are all closed when nesting wildlife is present.
  - Florida Keys Eco-Discovery Center is open from Tuesday to Saturday from 9 am to 4 pm.
  - Garden Key Visitor Center is open every day from 8:30 am to 4:30 pm.

- **Fees**

  - Entrance fees are valid for seven days:

    - $15 per person

- **Goods / Services**

  - There are no services on the islands and tourists need to be self-sufficient. It is important to note there is NO:

    - Cell phone coverage
    - Public phones
    - Internet
    - Bathrooms
    - Water

- ☐ Food
- ☐ Fuel
- ☐ Trashcans

☐ **Pets**

- ☐ Pets are allowed in the following areas:
  - ☐ Garden Key, but not inside Fort Jefferson

☐ **Camping**

- ☐ Camping is available at the Garden Key Campground. There are eight sites at $15 per night, and they are all first come, first served.

☐ **Reservations / Permits**

- ☐ Boat permits are required for private boats.

☐ **Wildlife**

- ☐ Perhaps the best opportunity available is to swim with sea turtles around the islands.
- ☐ In addition, the reefs are home to hundreds of species of sea life.
- ☐ Lastly, the islands are home to a number of bird species.

☐ **Weather**

- ☐ Before visiting, it is important you check the weather reports first.
- ☐ The islands typically experience two seasons: winter takes place from November through April, and summer is May through October.

- ☐ Winter features strong cold fronts, large swells, and windy conditions. This is an excellent time for bird watching, but definitely not for snorkeling or other water activities.
- ☐ Summer brings milder weather but is also when hurricanes are likely to happen.

☐ **When to Visit**

- ☐ Summer is the best time to visit, but check the weather forecast to avoid traveling during hurricanes.

☐ **Visiting Tips**

- ☐ Make sure to come prepared since there is no food or water on the island.
- ☐ Spring migration is the best time to see birds.
- ☐ It is well worth the extra money to take a seaplane tour.

BISCAYNE, FLORIDA

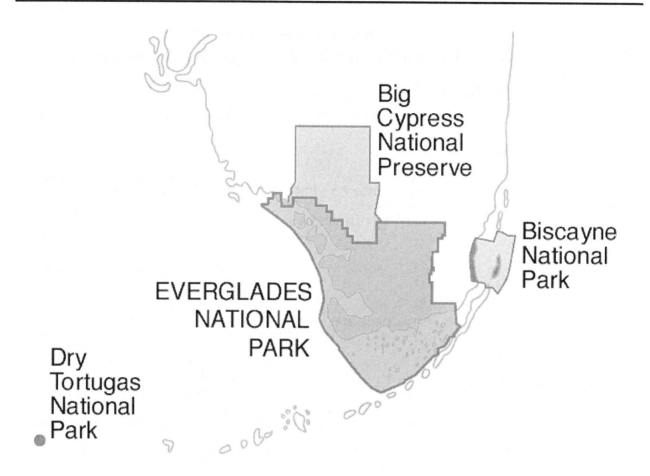

Overview

Near the bustling city of Miami, you'll find peace and quiet in the beautiful outdoors of Biscayne National Park. Within this park is Biscayne Bay, one of the top places for scuba diving in the world. In fact, nearly 90% of this National Park is water. It also encompasses a third-longest living coral reef in the world.

- **Visitor Centers / Hours**
    - The park is open year-round, but the hours per day may vary:
        - Dante Fascell Visitor Center is open every day from 9 am to 5 pm, except Christmas.

- Convoy Point Grounds is open daily from 7 am to 5:30 pm.
- Navigable waters and the accessible Elliott Key and Boca Chita Key are open 24 hours.
- Adams Key is a day-use only area.

- **Fees**
  - There are no entrance fees.

- **Goods / Services**
  - There are no goods or services available at the park.

- **Pets**
  - Pets on a leash not over six feet are allowed on the grounds around the Visitor Center and the developed Elliott Key.

- **Camping**
  - Camping is available at Elliott Key or Boca Chita Key at $25 per night. Docking space is first come, first served.

- **Reservations / Permits**
  - There are no reservations.

- **Wildlife**
  - The largest mammals in the area are the bobcat and white-tailed deer.
  - The rest of the mammals are of the smaller variety such as raccoons, opossums, rats, and squirrels.

- There is a wide range of aquatic species and birds to observe and bask in the loveliness of this destination.

- **Weather**

    - Dry season takes place from November to April, and wet season is from May to October.

- **When to Visit**

    - The best time to visit is in winter, due to the ironic tropical climate.
    - November through April is the best time to visit to see manatees.

- **Visiting Tips**

    - The reef is very vulnerable, so take precautions while you are snorkeling or when it comes to disposing of your garbage.
    - You'll need to make reservations for ranger-led tours, and they tend to fill up fast, so book in advance.

ACADIA, MAINE

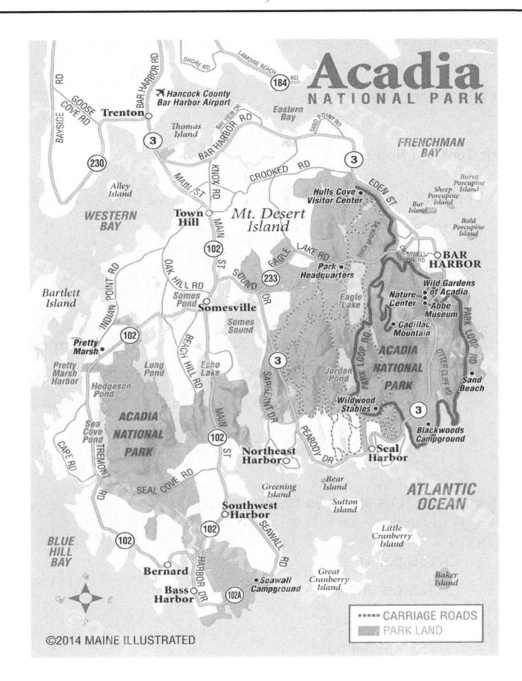

Overview

Acadia National Park is located along a cluster of islands on the jagged coast of Maine. Despite the remote location, there are several landscapes to explore including mountains, woodlands, lakes, ponds, and ocean beaches.

The park includes Cadillac Mountain, the tallest point on the Atlantic Coast at 1,530 feet. You have the unique opportunity to hike 45 miles of historic carriage roads that were built in the 19th and early 20th centuries. Acadia National Park was established in 1919 and was the first park settled on the east of the Mississippi River.

- **Visitor Centers / Hours**
    - The park is open year-round but may have inaccessible areas during the winter.
    - Hulls Cove Visitor Center:
        - April 15th to June 30th daily from 8:30 am to 4:30 pm
        - July 1st to September 3rd daily from 8 am to 6 pm
        - September 4th to October 31st daily from 8:30 am to 4:30 pm.
- **Fees**
    - Entrance fees are valid for seven days:
        - $30 per vehicle
        - $25 per motorcycle
        - $15 per person
        - $55 annual pass
- **Goods / Services**
    - Other than camping, there is no lodging in the park.
    - The only dining option is the Jordan Pond House Restaurant open mid-May to late October.
- **Pets**

- Pets on a leash not over six feet are allowed in campgrounds and on most hiking trails.

- **Camping**
    - Camping is available at four campsites throughout the park:
        - Blackwoods Campground. Open all year. $30 per campsite from May to October. April to November campsites are $15, weather permitting. December to March camping is primitive and by permit only.
        - Seawall Campground. Open from late May to late September. $22 for walk-in sites and $30 for drive-in sites.
        - Schoodic Woods Campground. Open late May to Columbus Day. Fees are $22 to $40 depending on the site.
        - Duck Harbor Campground on Isle Au Haut. Five primitive sites are accessible by boat from May 15th to October 15th.

- **Reservations / Permits**
    - Reservations are highly recommended, especially during peak visit times.

- **Wildlife**
    - The diverse nature of the park makes it home to over 1,500 species of plants, birds, and mammals.

- **Weather**

- The Gulf of Maine prevents the park from having terribly hot or freezing cold temperature ranges. The average temperature is about 45 degrees Fahrenheit.
- In the summer the water is cool, so the inland temperatures are lower than in other areas.

When to Visit

- You can visit the park year-round, but most people choose to go in the summer.
- Pack for all weather and dress in layers no matter what time of the year you choose to visit it.

Visiting Tips

- If you travel during the busy season of Memorial Day through fall, arrive early morning or late afternoon to avoid the majority of the crowds.
- The park has numerous hiking trails so be sure you buy a trail map and use it to carefully plan your route.

PART -2

WHAT TO SEE IN A DAY-TRIP

GUADALUPE MOUNTAINS, TEXAS

Guadalupe Mountains National Park is a wonderful place to visit, even if you only have a short time to spend. You can stop by the Pine Springs Visitor Center, where you can tour the museum and waterslide show.

From there you can head out on the Pinery Nature Trail, which is less than a mile of paved hiking with signs displaying facts about local plants that takes you to the historic 1858 Old Butterfield Stagecoach Route Pinery Station.

Another great option is the Smith Spring Trail at a 2.3-mile round-trip. This trail gives you some excellent views of the mountains and surrounding landscapes. Another option is the Devil's Hall Trail, a 4.3-mile round-trip. You will have to do some boulder scrambling, but it takes you to a natural staircase that forms a hallway between the canyon walls. Lastly, you can try the McKittrick Canyon Trail at a 5.7-mile round-trip for a chance to see some native wildlife.

If you have already visited and are looking for a hike to take you all day, consider a more isolated, longer hike. Some great options are the Guadalupe Peak Trail, the Bowl Trail, or the McKittrick Canyon Trail that leads you to the Grotto.

The Guadalupe Peak Trail is a challenging 8.5-mile hike. The trail will guide you up 3,000 feet to the top of the highest peak in Texas. From here, you can enjoy beautiful panoramic views of the desert and forest below.

Most people choose to explore the main trails within McKittrick Canyon. The best one to go for is the Permian Reef Trail. This is a quiet trail of 8.4 miles that allows you to experience all the park has to offer, from sheer cliff walls to desert plants. You'll also be able to see the remains of ancient ocean life etched into the soft limestone.

If you want to get away from the crowds for a day, head to Dog Canyon. This location is at the boundary of the wilderness and takes you to an elevation of 6,300 feet. There are three trails that walk you into this area: Indian Meadow Natural Trail, Marcus Overlook, and Lost Peak Trail.

You can choose to connect the Lost Peak Trail to the McKittrick Ridge Trail for a longer, more strenuous hike.

If you aren't in the mood to hike, stop by the historic Frijole and Williams Ranches. Another must-see stop is the Salt Basin Dunes.

Even though this park is small, there are dozens of attractions to observe; you may even want to combine this with the Big Bend National Park in Texas for an extended trip to see everything.

BIG BEND, TEXAS

If it is your first time visiting this National Park or if you simply don't have a lot of time, make sure you have a well-planned itinerary in place. Most people are surprised at the size of this park and the diverse range of opportunities it presents. To get the most out of your short trip here, consider this incoming two-week itinerary and listed activities you can do in a single day.

One of the best things you can do is drive the Ross Maxwell Scenic Drive with several stops along the way and an extended stop at the Chisos Basin and the Castolon Historic District.

The Ross Maxwell Scenic Drive is a 30-mile trip that takes you to Santa Elena Canyon and past various historical and geological features along the way. As you drive along this road, be sure to stop and stretch your legs at these following sites.

SAM NAIL RANCH

This is one of the original homesteads that was active in the area, and the current remnants are a great place to spot native wildlife. Take a moment to sit on a bench and listen for creatures scurrying in the brush or watch the many birds that hang out at the still-active windmill.

BLUE CREEK RANCH OVERLOOK

At this overlook, you can see the headquarters of the old Homer Wilson Ranch. You can take a short trail down to the ranch buildings and even hike further along the Blue Creek Canyon and Dodson trails if you want and have the time.

SOTOL VISTA OVERLOOK

This viewpoint is located above the desert floor and allows you to enjoy a beautiful vista of the western side of the National Park. You'll even be able to spot your destination of Santa Elena Canyon in the distance.

LOWER BURRO MESA POUROFF

This side road is only 1.5 miles off your main drive and takes you to the base of the colorful cliffs along Burro Mesa. From here you can hike a half-mile trail into a hidden box canyon with a dry waterfall. It is a worthwhile side-trip to take if you have the time since you can closely observe various species of desert plants and geological samples.

MULE EARS VIEWPOINT

From the parking area, you can view the Mule Ears Peaks, or you can get out and hike the short two-mile trail to a refreshing desert spring.

TUFF CANYON

This canyon is comprised of soft volcanic tuff or compressed ash. The canyon can be seen from two viewing platforms, or you can hike through the gorge.

CASTOLON HISTORIC DISTRICT

This area was first established as a cavalry camp in the early 20th century. Later, it became the headquarters for the La Harmonia Company. Today you can find a visitor center and camper store in the location with the nearby Cottonwood Campground.

SANTA ELENA CANYON

This is one of the greatest canyons in the park, standing at 1,500 feet of vertical limestone. As you contemplate the canyon, the left side covers the beginning of Mexico and the right side is in Texas. You can hike a trail that follows the river upstream, then heads down toward the crackling canyon floor.

If you still have time left in the day, head to the Chisos Mountains. Take the short 0.3-mile Window View Trail to bask in the beauty of the outstanding mountain scenery. You can get even closer if you choose to continue the hike along Window Trail or Lost Mine Trail.

BADLANDS, SOUTH DAKOTA

The Badlands National Park offers you plenty of opportunities for discovery and outdoor exploration. Whether you want to camp for several days or a simple day visit of driving through the park, you'll find thousands of outdoor activities to keep you busy.

If it is your first time visiting the park, you should consider stopping by the Ben Reifel Visitor Center. Here you'll be able to watch the film 'Land of Stone and Light' in a new 95-seat, air-conditioned theater. There are also interactive exhibits focusing on the local cultural history, the ecology of the prairie, and the paleontology surrounding the creatures frozen in time within the limestone.

For children, there are activities such as assembling a virtual dinosaur skeleton or handling fossilized animal casts.

You may be able to take delight in the paleontology lab set up in the Ben Reifel Visitor Center during certain times of the year; it all depends on when you arrive at the park. The Fossil Preparation Lab is a fully functional laboratory that allows visitors to watch licensed paleontologists work while learning about the scientific discoveries being made. It is open daily from 9 am to 4:30 pm starting in the second week in June until the third week in September.

One of the most popular activities at this park is hiking. There are several short, easy trail options to choose from if your visit is quick. Consider some of these short hiking trail options.

The Fossil Exhibit Trail is a 0.25-mile round-trip. It is an easily-accessible boardwalk trail that takes you past fossil replicas and exhibits of extinct creatures that once roamed that very land.

Cliff Shelf is a moderately difficult half-mile round-trip trail. It is a boardwalk loop trail that climbs through a juniper forest along the wall of the Badlands. The entire trail goes up about 200 feet in elevation, and there is the chance you'll see deer or sheep drinking water at one of the many clear ponds along the way.

Saddle Pass is a short yet strenuous 0.25-mile round-trip. The trail guides you up the Badlands Wall where you can bask in a panoramic scene of the White River Valley below. The trail ends when it connects to the Castle and Medicine Root Loop Trails.

The Door Trail is an easy 0.75-mile round-trip. This is an accessible boardwalk trail that takes covers a break in the Badlands Wall called the Door so that you can get a beautiful view of the Badlands. You can choose to travel beyond this maintained trail if you want to go off on your own quest for nature and solitude.

The Window Trail is a simple 0.25-mile round-trip. This is another trail that takes you to a natural window in the Badlands Wall where you can really absorb the intricate canyon.

Lastly, there is the 1.5-mile round-trip Notch Trail. This hike is moderate to strenuous, so only attempt it in a day if you are in good physical shape. After hiking through the canyon, the trail climbs a log ladder to a ledge known as the Notch.

It is at this ledge where you can have breathtaking vistas of the White River Valley. The trail isn't recommended for those who have a fear of heights. Avoid it during the summer, as it can be dangerous in times of heavy rains.

WIND CAVE, SOUTH DAKOTA

Most people come to the park for the cave, and there are several guided tour options that you can do in a day. However, if going underground isn't your thing, you can also choose to do several day activities above ground as well. Let's take a look at your options.

Perhaps the easiest cave tour you can take is the Garden of Eden Tour, which is ideal for those short on time or those with physical limitations. The tour is an hour and allows you to experience everything in the cave system. You enter and leave the cave through an elevator, after which point you only have to go up 150 steps during the actual tour.

Another option is the Natural Entrance Tour. While you can't enter the cave through the 18-inch natural entrance, you will get a chance to see it. This tour is moderately complicated, as it does require you to go through narrow passages and climb about 300 stairs, most of them headed downhill. The tour is a little over an hour long and covers about two-thirds of a mile.

Above ground, you'll definitely want to make time for a scenic drive through the park. However, be prepared to be patient, since bison herds tend to stand on the roads and impede traffic. If you need to, get out of the car and stretch your legs at one of the many trails available in the park.

There are several easy trails that are a mile or less and will give you a taste of the area without taking up much of your day. The best hike for extended sights is the Rankin Ridge, which takes you to the highest point in the park.

THEODORE ROOSEVELT, NORTH DAKOTA

Theodore Roosevelt consists of a booming 70,447 acres found on the western edge of the state of North Dakota. The park is divided into three units: North, South, and Elkhorn Ranch. Let's look at what you can do at each unit in this park.

SOUTH UNIT

The main feature of the South Unit is the 36-mile long Scenic Loop Drive. Along the way, you can enjoy pullouts and interpretive signs that explain more about the park, as well as wide open views of prairies, wildflowers, and gentle wildlife.

Just inside the park entrance you also want to stop at the South Unit Visitor Center near the town of Medora. Here you can watch a park film and tour a museum that tells you fun facts about that destination. Next, to the visitor center, you'll be able to see the Maltese Cross Cabin, the first ranch cabin of Roosevelt.

Elkhorn Ranch Unit

This unit helps protect the location of Roosevelt's home ranch within the Badlands. The only remains of the buildings are the stone foundations. In order to access this site, you'll need to drive over gravel roads for 35 miles. It is recommended that you have a high-clearance vehicle before attempting this trip.

North Unit

This unit of the park is located near Watford City about 50 miles from the park entrance. The Visitor Center also features exhibits and a park film. There is a 14-mile Scenic Drive that takes you to the Oxbow Overlook, with turnouts and interpretive signs along the way.

The most common way to experience Theodore Roosevelt National Park is by taking one of the two scenic drives in either the South or North Units. If you only have a day or less, it is recommended to take the Southern Unit drive.

If you can stay the entire day, head toward the Boicourt Overlook in the South Unit at sunset, when the sky looks as though it has caught on fire, accompanied by pink and purple clouds in the horizon. An easy 15-minute trail takes you along the ridge of a small mountain to an overlook.

Hiking Options

You can also hike the area for a little bit. The following are some of your trail options:

Easy Trails

- Skyline Vista - South Unit - 0.1 miles
- Boicourt Overlook Trail - South Unit - 0.2 miles
- Little Mo Trail - North Unit - 0.7 to 1.1 miles, depending on loop
- Buck Hill - South Unit - 0.2 miles
- Wind Canyon Trail - South Unit - 0.4 miles

Moderate Trails

- Ridgeline Trail - South Unit - 0.6 miles
- Coal Vein Trail - South Unit - 0.6 to 0.8 miles, depending on loop
- Painted Canyon Nature Trail - South Unit - 0.9 miles
- Caprock Coulee Nature Trail - North Unit - 1.5 miles
- Prairie Dog Town via the Buckhorn Trail - North Unit - 1.5 miles
- Sperati Point via the Achenbach Trail - North Unit - 1.5 miles

Strenuous Trails

- Caprock Coulee - North Unit - 4.3 miles
- Maah Daah Hey - South Unit - 7.1 miles
- Lone Tree Loop - South Unit - 9.6 miles
- Petrified Forest Loop - South Unit - 10.3 miles
- Buckhorn - North Unit - 11.4 miles
- Jones/Lower Talkington/Lower Paddock Loop - South Unit - 11.4 miles
- Upper Paddock/Talkington Loop - South Unit - 15.4 to 19.4 miles, depending on the route
- Achenbach - North Unit - 18 miles

VOYAGEURS, MINNESOTA

Water-based activities are the most popular at Voyageurs, largely due to the 344 square miles of water. The bulk of summer activities include boating, canoeing, kayaking, swimming, and fishing. Stop in at any of the three visitor centers to learn about guided tours of the islands or to rent a boat to head out on the water yourself.

Perhaps the most visited destination in the park is the Kabetogama Peninsula. You can only access this area by boat in the summer and snowmobile in the winter. Here you want to take a stroll around the Ellsworth Rock Art Sculpture Garden on the south shore.

If you want to get a glimpse of the local wildlife, then head out on the Cruiser Lake Trail. This area offers you your best chance to encounter moose. The full trail is a strenuous 9.5-mile one-way hike that takes you through wetlands and over rocky cliffs, but you can choose to turn back at a variety of loops and only hike as far as you can in a day.

For a more relaxed wildlife-viewing experience consider the easy Echo Bay Trail, a 2.5-mile hike known for birdwatching. You'll be able to see a blue heron rookery with binoculars, as well as various other birds. Plus, you have the chance to spot deer as well. Keep in mind this trail can get quite muddy in wet weather. In the winter, the trail is groomed for cross-country skiing.

If you want a more remote and private experience head for the Blind Ash Bay Trail, this moderate 2.5-mile loop trail can be hiked in the summer and snowshoed in the winter. The trail takes you through forests and offers a range of wildlife-viewing opportunities.

Just because winter brings snow, it doesn't mean you can't visit the park and have fun outdoors. In the winter, the park has both groomed and ungroomed trails for cross-country skiing and snowshoeing no matter what your skill level might be. Most winter trails are accessible from Ash River or Rainy Lake visitor centers.

The park is also one of the only National Parks in the lower 48 states that allows snowmobiling in the winter with over 110 miles of maintained trails.

ISLE ROYALE, MICHIGAN

Isle Royale is a National Park that is only accessible by boat or float plane and is the only National Park that fully closes throughout the winter. The park is only open from May to September. You'll need to do some effort and advanced planning to make a trip to the island. Most people choose to spend the night there, but it is possible to see the majority of the island on a day trip.

While you may feel you are confined to a relatively small island with not much room for exciting possibilities and activities, there are actually 165 miles of trails to explore and enjoy. Most hikes start at either the Windigo Visitor Center on the southwestern end of the island or from the Rock Harbor Visitor Center on the northeastern end.

From the southwestern side, consider the six-mile round-trip Minong Ridge Trail that provides you with a challenging hike among rocky ledges, forests, and marshes in the company of moose and beavers.

There is a viewpoint along the way from which you can check out the Canadian shoreline. The entire trail can be extended to 26 miles to McCargoe Cove for those who want a multi-day backpacking adventure.

On the northeastern end of the island, there is a unique experience waiting for you in the Ojibway Fire Tower. It is either a 3.5-mile round-trip or a 5.1-mile look that starts at the Daisy Farm Campground. This trail climbs several ridges and takes you to the highest point on the eastern end of the island.

If hiking isn't your thing, you can also choose to dive into the waters surrounding the island. In fact, that are 25 major haunting shipwrecks within Lake Superior. Ten of these sites are explorable by scuba diving.

You can do so on your own or through one of several operators in the area. Just be prepared for very cold water.

The most popular wreck is The America; the ship was beached in 1928, and today you can swim in nearly all portions of the wreck including the crew quarters, galley, ballroom, and engine room.

CUYAHOGA VALLEY, OHIO

There are plenty of ways to address the many tourist destinations in Cuyahoga Valley National Park and being that it is so close to two major cities. You can easily explore parts of the park on a day trip or come back for extra days to see multiple parts you might have missed after spending a night relaxing in a room along with warm food. You are sure to find something to do at this park.

One of the most hiked trails in the park is the Brandywine Gorge Trail, a 1.5-mile loop that allows you to explore Brandywine Creek with views of Brandywine Falls, a 65-foot bridal veil waterfall. The loop takes you up 160 feet from start to finish and is best for those who are used to moderate to strenuous trails.

Another popular trail in the park is the Ohio and Erie Canal Towpath Trail that takes you through the entire park. This is a level trail that follows the historic route of the Ohio & Erie Canal. The entire trail is 20 miles, but you can hike a large portion in a day. The path also connects with several stops on the Cuyahoga Valley Scenic Railroad.

If you're short on time, go on the half-mile route from Buckeye Trail to Blue Hen Falls. This trail goes up 80 feet and takes you through tall grasses and magnificent oak trees. In the end, you reach an overhanging plate of sandstone with a small stream and a 15-foot waterfall.

The 2.2-mile long Ledges Trail is the most recommended during the cold season, partly because it not only allows you to see crystal clear icicle formations on the rocks but also incomparable panoramas of a snow-ridden winter wonderland across the valley. You'll also have a chance to inspect the Ice Box Cave and its petroglyphs dating back to the 1900s. The Towpath Trail is also a great spot for cross-country skiing.

Just north of the Ira Trailhead, you can check out the beaver marsh. You will be able to see both their half-built and finished dams, and if you approach the marsh in the mid-evening, you could catch them adding the final touches. Aside from beavers, bird-watchers will have a field day at this location, since there are dozens of bird species waiting to be photographed.

For fans of the Great Blue Heron: the park has two sanctuaries where you may see both the heron and its babies during March or April. The 2.75-mile loop called Tree Farm Trail also allows you to observe the wildlife from a closer point.

Unique hiking experience is the portion of the Buckeye Trail that travels through the park. This trail is a 1,400-mile loop that circles the state. Between Station Road Bridge and Boston, the trail covers 12.6 miles in the park. Boston is a historic village that is still home to 1,300 people.

If you don't have enough time to take a hike, but still want to see as much of the park as possible then consider a unique alternative solution. The Cuyahoga Valley Scenic Railroad runs through the park. You can get an all-day pass and get on and off the train as often as you want so you can explore various parts without doing so much leg-work.

GATEWAY ARCH, MISSOURI

No visit to this park is complete without touring the iconic Gateway Arch. Built about 50 years ago, this monument was designed by architect Eero Saarinen to commemorate the vision of Thomas Jefferson and the role St. Louis played in the westward expansion of the United States.

Definitely schedule in time to take a tram ride to the top of the Arch and enjoy panoramic views of the St. Louis area below you. The tram system is unique to the Arch and takes you on a 630-foot ride to the top.

If you're afraid of heights or don't have the time to schedule a tram ride to the top, stop by the museum located under the Gateway Arch. This museum teaches you about westward expansion and the role St. Louis played in this important event in history. While at the museum you could see the film "Monument to the Dream" that shows you how the Arch was constructed.

Another unique method to admire the Arch is to take one of the many Riverboat Cruise options along the Mississippi River. Or, for the more adventurous sort, you can even schedule a helicopter ride to take you above the Arch for a truly unique perspective.

Once you've visited the Arch, head to the Old Courthouse, here, you can see the restored courtrooms where important cases– such as the Dred Scott case in 1847 and 1850– were held. It was also the place where the women's right to vote came on trial in the 1870s.

The Old Courthouse is also listed in the National Park Service's National Underground Railroad Network to Freedom. This recognizes sites, programs, and facilities that were associated with the Underground Railroad.

HOT SPRINGS, ARKANSAS

While it is considered one of the smallest parks at only 5,550 acres, Hot Springs National Park still defends itself with its varied attractions. For one, the park is mandated to give away their main natural resource free to the public: the mineral water.

Unlike what you might expect at other National Parks, the most popular activity here happens indoors. At the Buckstaff you'll find the only operational bath house within a National Park that has been operating continuously since 1912. There are a few options to choose from, but the most well-known is the Whirlpool Mineral Bath.

This process involves a soak in a 110-degree tub; a loofah scrubs down, another soak in a tub with hot water poured down on you, sitting in a sauna, a hot pack wrap, and a brief time in a "needle shower." If this doesn't sound appealing to you, there are three outdoor pools where you can enjoy the 143-degree water without any extra scrubbing or treatment.

If you prefer to stay dry while visiting the park, pack a lunch and head out for a scenic drive. There are two popular mountain drives that offer you fantastic panoramic views.

You can also pay a fee to climb to the top of the observation tower on Hot Springs Mountain, or perhaps a picnic at the Grand Promenade, Hot Springs Mountain, West Mountain, and Gulpha Gorge Overlooks.

Not to mention, there are still 26 miles of hiking trails to give you plenty of single day-hiking options. The only trail that may take you all day is the Sunset Trail, a 10-mile adventure that is often broken into three shorter hikes. The first section is the most popular route on West Mountain that is close to town and amenities for those passing through.

The second route takes you through forests on Sugarloaf Mountain and faces Balanced Rock. The last section goes through Stonebridge Road and what was once the Fordyce family estate; this area is known for wildflowers and shy forest animals.

A favorite hike among locals is the 1.7-mile Hot Springs Mountain Trail. This easy to moderate trail climbs through a forest with spectacular vistas along the way. Another option is the 1.6-mile Dead Chief Trail going from Bathhouse Row to Gulpha Gorge Campground.

The route starts off steep but later levels off and takes you across the south slope of Hot Springs Mountain. A portion follows the historic "fitness trail" that was a part of the healing regime at the resort in the 1900s.

Hot Springs also has its own brewery inside the park borders. Stop by the Superior Bathhouse Brewery to try a flight of beer made from the thermal waters.

If you travel at the right time, make it a point to bring a basket. The park is plentiful in fruits and nuts you can glean while in season. This includes plums, blackberries, hickory nuts, persimmons, grapes, muscadines, blueberries, and juneberries. The National Park allows you to collect for personal consumption only.

While you can easily enjoy the highlights of this park in as little as three to four hours, you'll likely want to stay longer.

If you do, it is highly recommended you head outside the park and check out the attractions offered in the historic town of Hot Springs.

GREAT SMOKY MOUNTAINS, TENNESSEE, AND NORTH CAROLINA

The Great Smoky Mountains is a huge National Park that takes on two states and is over a half million acres. Seeing the entire park or even a decent portion of it in a single day is a daunting task.

So it is best to simply choose an activity that interests you and find the best way to go through it. After all, you may return at a later occasion.

Perhaps the best way to tackle most of the park in a single day is to take an auto tour. The National Park features over 270 miles of roads, and while most the roads are paved, even gravel roads are maintained in suitable enough condition for most two-wheel drive vehicles. If you are going to auto tour the park there are four highly recommended drives to take.

First is the 33-mile Newfound Gap Road.

This highway uses the Newfound Gap at 5,046 feet to connect Cherokee, North Carolina to Gatlinburg, Tennessee. There are many pull-outs along the way that provide you with breathtaking views and plentiful forests as you climb the 3,500 feet to crest the mountain.

A second option is Clingmans Dome Road, open April 1st to November 30th. It is a seven-mile spur road that follows a high ridge. In the end, you can take a 0.5-mile paved hiking trail to the highest peak in the park.

Another option is the 18-mile Little River Road, which goes alongside the river from Sugarland Visitor Center to Townsend, Tennessee. Along the way, you can enjoy cooling misty waterfalls and sweet-scented wildflowers.

Lastly, consider the short six-mile long Roaring Fork Motor Nature Trail. It is open from March 25th to November 30th. The road is steep and narrow, so no buses or RVs are allowed. Along the way, you will come across more forests and historic, quaint farmsteads.

If you have time to get out and explore the park on foot, there are plenty of outdoor activities. Consider taking a ranger-guided hike, a horseback ride, a hayride, or a bicycle ride.

Be sure to pack a lunch and make a day of it with an afternoon stop for a picnic. There are plenty of picnic areas to choose from throughout the park while you take delight in the beautiful scenery around you.
You'll likely enjoy the park so much that you'll want to return later and make a longer trip out of it.

CONGAREE, SOUTH CAROLINA

There are plenty of ways to have a fantastic time at Congaree National Park in South Carolina, whether it is taking a short stroll along the boardwalk or canoeing down Cedar Creek. Come see what you can explore in the National Park that is home to one of the oldest and tallest forests east of the Mississippi.

Since most of the Congaree trails are in a floodplain, they are often flat terrain. At the eastern section of the park, you can hike the two-mile round-trip Bates Ferry Trail following the historic ferry road used to take people and supplies to South Carolina's cities. The trail ends at Bates Ferry landing where you can overlook the Congaree River.

Another option is to take the 1.3-mile Sims Trail that follows an old gravel road from the Bluff Trail south to Cedar Creek. This hike is a great place to spot wildlife such as the box turtle, fox squirrel, deer, and multiple types of birds.

Nearby, you can also choose the Bluff Trail: a 1.7-mile trail that loops north of the visitor center and leads you through a prime example of the forests the park is known for. It also gains you access to two camping areas.

If you want to see otters and other wading birds like storks and herons, you'll want to head out on the Weston Lake Loop Trail. This 4.4-mile path guides you near Cedar Creek and a dried-up riverbed surrounded by cypress trees.

For those who love to photograph old growth trees, there is the 6.6 mile Oakridge Trail, where you're likely to spot deer and wild turkey. The road connects the Kingslake and River trails. The Kingsnake Trail is a valuable 11.7-mile option for bird watchers since it takes you near Cedar Creek and is a popular pitstop for many bird species.

You could kayak or canoe the Cedar Creek as well, which is about 15 miles long, starts at Bannister's Bridge, and ends at the Congaree River. From your kayak or canoe, you have the chance to spot deer and friendly river otters. If you aren't familiar with canoeing, you can take a ranger-guided canoe tour.

Another unique route takes the Big Tree Hike. This is a five-mile, off-trail hike led by a volunteer naturalist, as well as a great way to see parts of the park that you wouldn't otherwise be able to reach.
When visiting in May and June be sure to stay after dark to marvel at dozens of synchronized lightning bugs. This is one of the few accessible locations in the United States where you can see these bugs light up in unison instead of sporadically. This is a once-in-a-lifetime experience you won't get anywhere else.

MAMMOTH CAVE, KENTUCKY

Mammoth Cave National Park is home to one of the largest cave systems in the world at over 365 miles and five levels that have been mapped with tons still to be investigated. However, there is much more to this park than the cave system. Above ground, there are 52,800 acres of forest with two rivers. You'll have a hard time deciding what to do on a day trip to this park and may decide you want to stay for a longer period of time.

Millions visit this park every year for the sole purpose of going to the cave system. If you plan to take a cave tour, you should pre-book in advance since the guided tours tend to fill up quickly. There are various tours to choose from so be sure to pick one that meets your time needs as well as your fitness level. If you are visiting the park with small children or if you don't like the idea of navigating a lot of stairs then you should consider the Frozen Niagara Tour. It takes just a little more than an hour and provides some of the best formations in the entire cave system. Even claustrophobic individuals can take this tour since it sticks to the larger caverns.

Another popular tour is the moderately difficult Domes and Dripstones Tour that takes two hours. It combines with the Frozen Niagara Tour and goes further to show you even more dramatic cave features. The difficult portion of the tour is over 500 stairs you need to climb and several tight areas that require some squeezing or ducking.

For the most adventurous sort, you should consider the Wild Cave Tour. This is a strenuous tour that is six hours long and covers five miles in the cave. This tour is limited to small groups and will have you scramble, crawl, squeeze and hike into the depths of the cave. You will be provided with caving equipment and outerwear for this tour.

Above ground, the park is divided in half by the Green River which runs east to west. The south side of the park is the Frontcountry portion, while the north side is the backcountry. In the Frontcountry you will find countless short and easy hikes you can do based on your time and interest. One of the most popular is the Cedar Sink Trail that features blooming wildflowers and a sinkhole.

The most well-known long distance hike of the park is the McCoy Hollow Trail. The trail starts at the Temple Hill parking area and covers six miles of hollows, ridges, and streams. It is one-way and can be done as an all-day hike or as an overnight backcountry hike.

In the summer months, you can take sightseeing tours on the Green River via a number of local providers by motorboat, canoe, or kayak. When you take a tour of the river, you'll be able to view a variety of formations as well as several wildlife species.

SHENANDOAH, VIRGINIA

Many visitors to Shenandoah looking to just visit for the day choose to tour Skyline Drive. This is especially true in October when the fall foliage is in the full-color mode. Skyline Drive is known as a National Scenic Byway and guides you along the top of the Blue Ridge Mountains for 105 miles.

The speed limit here is strictly enforced, so the entire drive takes about three hours one-way at 35 miles per hour. This leisure pace allows you to enjoy the beauty all around you on a nice, peaceful drive.

When you are ready to get out and stretch your legs, there are several options within the park. Perhaps the most popular trail in maybe the entire mid-Atlantic region is the nine-mile hike to the summit of Old Rag Mountain at 3,291 feet.

The last mile of this hike can be tough for the casual hiker. Along the way, you get to go through a natural cave and staircase. This is one of the few hikes in the park that isn't accessed by Skyline Drive. It is best to arrive before 7 am if you want to beat the crowds.

If you want an easier but equally rewarding hike, then consider the Hawksbill trail. This 2.9-mile round-trip only gains 860 feet of elevation and allows you to hike a short portion of the Appalachian Trail. Towards the top, you'll find a great rest spot with a view of a stone hut with a picnic table.

If you are more inclined toward a waterfall-related escapade, consider the White Oak Canyon area of the park. Here the standard loop trail is 9.1 miles and climbs to about 2,560 feet elevation.

It takes you through shady hemlock groves and passes eight waterfalls. You can adjust the distance to 4.6 miles if you only want to see the upper falls or you can do an extended 12-mile loop to the summit of Hawksbill.

In total, the National Park has over 500 miles of hiking trails and 40 percent of the park is designated wilderness. However, the best way to experience the park is by hiking a portion of the longest portion of the Appalachian Trail, standing at 101 miles.

In order to hike the entire length, it would take you 5 to 13 days depending on your hiking speed. It is important to note that this portion of the trail doesn't have any streams to cross so you'll need to carry your own water and add mileage if you leave the trail to find a water source.

EVERGLADES, FLORIDA

The Everglades is a huge park to visit, but there are actually few designated paths and trails to take. While the best way to have an adventure in the park is to plan a multi-day backcountry experience, there are still a few things you can do to enjoy a single day or short visit.

At opposite ends of the park, there are two easy, paved trails that give you a nice introduction to the Everglades and the biodiversity it contains. In the northern part of the park, you can start at the Shark Valley Visitor Center and hike or tram-ride to an observation tour that overlooks the Shark River Slough. From here you'll usually be able to see plenty of wildlife, particularly in the drier times of the year.

At the other end, in the southeast, you can take the Anhinga Trail through marshes and willow/pond-apple swamps until you reach the Taylor Slough just a few miles from the park headquarters. During the dry season, you'll encounter alligators and various bird species.

Nearby you can also take the Gumbo Limbo Trail if you have time. Both are easy, paved footpaths. The Gumbo Limbo Trail takes you through the Royal Palm Hammock and is one of the best ways to experience the Everglades jungle.

There is less wildlife to see here, but the botanical features are beautiful. Interpretive signs will help you identify trees in this area, including the gumbo limbo tree itself.

DRY TORTUGAS, FLORIDA

There are two main reasons why people visit Dry Tortugas National Park: they either come for the marine life, and the crystal waters with a pristine reef or they come for Fort Jefferson. This destination is still one of the lesser frequented ones in the National Park system and is a great place to enjoy nature while avoiding crowds.

The main challenge is getting out to the island. A boat trip takes about two and a half hours while a plane trip takes about 35 minutes. A ferry ticket is about $175, and a plane ride can be about $317. However, those who visit the island say it is very much worth the cost. Oftentimes, the fee will include a tour of the fort and a meal.

At Fort Jefferson, you can take a ranger-guided tour and learn about the fort's history. There is also a nice picnic area where you can enjoy lunch. Climbing to the third floor of the fort can give you some breathtaking views.

You can rent a kayak in Key West to bring across on the ferry. You will need to get a free boating permit. On a shorter trip, you can paddle around Garden Key, Bush Key, and Long Key or you can head three miles out to Loggerhead Key. Loggerhead Key is a great place for snorkeling and often has empty beaches that are quiet. However, this trip isn't for beginners since it takes open water with strong currents.

The best way to see the reefs and marine life is by getting in the water and doing some diving or snorkeling. Dry Tortugas has several site options, but just make sure you don't touch the coral and keep your distance from the sea turtles. The best spot for water activities is Windjammer, a shipwreck from 1901.

A calmer and protected shallow off Loggerhead Key is known as Little Africa is another great option with the chance to see barracuda and lobster. If you want to see a wide range of coral, then head to Texas Rock off Garden Key. The eastern boundary of the park is Pulaski Shoals Area, and it features many shipwrecks as well as sharks, eagle rays, and large grouper.

Back on land, the primary wildlife is birds; in fact, Dry Tortugas is home to 299 documented species. You'll even have a chance to view birds that don't nest anywhere else in the United States.

BISCAYNE, FLORIDA

Biscayne National Park is a beautiful park to visit, as it comes equipped with four distinct ecosystems: the mangrove swamp near the shore, the shallow Biscayne Bay, the coral keys, and the offshore reef. Within these ecosystems, there is a variety of animals, including over 200 species of fish and sixteen endangered species.

If you only have a day to visit, then you should start at the visitor center to learn about the park and area and then consider heading out on a ranger-led tour or a glass-bottom boat tour to get the best experience. If you have more time or prefer to venture out on your own, then there are a few other options to consider.

Much of the park is underwater, and as a result, the main activities that tourists enjoy are snorkeling and kayaking. The best spots for canoeing and kayaking is along the shoreline and in the shallow bay. The water the bay is only four to 10 feet deep, so you'll easily spot marine life in the clear water.

If you are more adventurous in your water activities, consider the seven-mile paddle across Biscayne Bay to Elliot, Boca Chita, or Adams Key. Most of these places aren't accessible by motorized boats so that you will have a peaceful and quiet experience. There are multiple paddling trails to enjoy in the park, and you'll be able to find one based on your skill and experience level.

Snorkeling along the shore isn't recommended since the mangrove is shallow and often filled with seagrass. The best way to snorkel is to take a tour or kayak at least 10 miles to the coral reef. There are tours that take you out to the reef, either offered by the park or by private companies.

If you want to see shipwrecks, you should take a ranger-led tour of the Maritime Heritage Trail. The Mandalay shipwreck has shallow and clear water with places to watch tropical fish. There are other shipwrecks that you can explore with full scuba gear.

If you want to stay on land, explore Elliot Key. This island has a six-mile-long trail running the length that includes a sub-tropical forest with birds, butterflies, and a unique variety of plants. There is also a swimming area near the key, as well as camping in designated areas in case you want to spend extra time here.

ACADIA, MAINE

Acadia National Park features over 127 miles of hiking trails so you can easily find something that matches your physical needs with your time.

Ocean Path is a moderate, 4.4-mile hike that offers plenty of scenic stops. This trail mostly follows Park Loop Road. You can start at Sand Beach, and the trail will take you to Thunder Hole by Monument Cove, through a forest and finally by the Otter Cliffs.

You can then choose to hike back or catch the Island Explorer for a ride to a new location. If you want an easier hike then simply follow Jordan Pond Path that takes you along the shores of Jordan Pond.

If you prefer to bike, the carriage roads are a great option in Arcadia. These rustic roads cover 45 miles around mountains and valleys, allowing bikers of all skill levels a chance to enjoy scenic views. You can also enjoy these roads for hiking or by horseback. If you don't have your own horse, you can rent one from Wildwood Stables.

Another way to explore the park is by bringing or renting a sea kayak or canoe and visiting the Porcupine Islands to explore the coastline. You can also choose to join a guided trip.

Many tourists falsely believe that Sand Beach is the only beach in the park. However, Echo Lake Beach is another option for sunbathing and swimming. This lake has slightly warmer water than Sand Beach. Both lakes are staffed with lifeguards in the summer months. Another popular alternative is Little Hunters Beach, but it has no lifeguards on call and fewer crowds.

In the winter months, the carriage roads of the park are groomed for cross-country skiing and snowshoeing. You can also take your snowmobile along Park Loop Road or up to Cadillac Mountain. Other options during this time are hiking, ice fishing, and camping.

If you want a less congested visit to the park, then head to the Schoodic Peninsula. This area has a new trail system and is only an hour drive from Bar Harbor or a one hour ferry and Island Explorer ride in peak season.

If you prefer to view the park from your vehicle, you can drive the scenic Park Loop Road along the coastline for a fantastic 27 miles of viewpoints. The road starts at Hulls Cove Visitor Center and branches off into access to points such as Sand Beach, Thunder Hole, Otter Cliffs, Jordan Pond, and Cadillac Mountain. To avoid crowds, it is a good idea to head to the top of Cadillac Mountain before 11 am or after 4 pm.

Another driving option is to take a two and a half hour narrated bus tour. There are three 15 minute stops. These tours occur from May to October.

PART – 3
14-DAY PARK HOPPER TRAVEL PLANS

Two-Week Trip Itineraries

If you have two weeks to spare and want to take an in-depth trip of any of the mentioned National Parks, there are some things you need to see. There are three sets of two-week trip itineraries to give you an idea of how you can spend a wonderful mini vacation drowning in the sheer Thoreau-inspired beauty of the wild.

ITINERARY #1: TEXAS

THE GUADALUPE MOUNTAINS AND BIG BEND

These two parks may be combined for a nice two-week trip. Spend a week at each or make adjustments based on your itinerary needs. The Guadalupe Mountains is a smaller park, and you may not need a whole week there, but Big Bend is a huge park that will need a lot of time to run through. Consider some of your options and design an itinerary that works for you.

GUADALUPE MOUNTAINS

Guadalupe Mountains National Park is a paradise for the hiker– with over 80 miles of trails that take you through woodland canyons and springs or into the rugged wilderness. If you aren't into hiking, there are several other options you can enjoy.

You could go backpacking into the rugged wilderness, or sit quietly and observe birds and other animals. No matter what activities you choose, your base will be the Pine Springs Campground with 20 tent and RV sites.

McKittrick Canyon

Tucked into a canyon with 2,000-foot high limestone walls and sometimes referred to as the most beautiful area in Texas. McKittrick Creek creates the winding path of the canyon that is home to a variety of plants and animals. This area of the park is certainly a must-see, especially when the fall colors are at full beauty in a whirlwind of reds and burning oranges.

Frijole Ranch

At one time the area was the main headquarters for ranching in the Guadalupe, now it is home to the Frijole Ranch History Museum. This museum shows you the history of humans in the Guadalupe from the Native Americans and ranchers to modern-day park activities.

You can also check out a one-room schoolhouse. This is the best way to experience what life was like in this remote part of West Texas in the early days of settlement.

Dog Canyon

Dog Canyon is in a secluded and forested location at the north and sits at an elevation of 6,300 feet. This is perhaps the furthest you can get from civilization while staying at the park. It is a great place for quiet camping, birding, and hiking for those who want true solitude on their vacation.

Williams Ranch

There is a 7.5-mile road that leads to this section of the park, and a part of it follows the old Butterfield Overland Mail stage route. The road ends abruptly at a 3,000-foot cliff on the west of the Guadalupe Mountains. Here, you'll find a well-preserved abandoned house. After this point, you can explore Bone Canyon, home to some of the oldest rocks in the Guadalupe.

Salt Basin Dunes

This section of the park covers about 2,000 acres and contains everything from vegetated three-foot mounts to 60-foot barren dunes. There are plenty of places to bask in the outdoors and get away from it all. Speak with personnel at the Pine Springs Visitor Center about how to visit this area of the park.

Once you have finished spending as much time as you need to adequately explore as much of Guadalupe Mountains National Park as you wish, you can head off to the second part of your trip. Big Bend National Park is so big you'll need at least a week here to open all the possibilities of exploration.

BIG BEND

With at least a week to visit Big Bend National Park, you'll be able to explore most of it and experience all it has to offer. You'll be able to hike and drive most of the routes available. Just remember, that for some of the "unimproved" dirt roads you'll need a high-clearance vehicle and possibly even a four-wheel drive. Any visitor center can give you information on current road conditions.

Start your week off with some scenic drives to get a feel for the environment of the park. There are 100 miles of paved roads and 150 miles of dirt roads that offer you a great way to explore the park from the comfort of your vehicle.

PAVED SCENIC DRIVES

Chisos Basin Road - six miles

The best way to experience how the park transitions from scorching desert to a cool mountain habitat. This scenic drive rises 2,000 feet above the desert and provides you an overlook of mountain peaks above the erosion-formed basin.

The road was first built by the Civilian Conservation Corps in the 1930s. It is not recommended to take the drive with a trailer longer than 20 feet or an RV over 24 feet since it features sharp curves and steep grades up to 15 percent.

Once you reach Chisos Basin, there is a visitor center, campground, lodge, restaurant, camp store, and miles' worth of hiking trails.

Ross Maxwell Scenic Drive - 30 miles

Taking a drive along this route will showcase the geological wonders of this park. The road has many scenic overlooks and exhibits that you can stop to learn more about the park. Three top must-see stops are the Sotol Vista, Mule Ears Overlook, and Tuff Canyon. This route also takes you by Sam Nail Ranch, Homer Wilson Ranch, and the Castolon Historic Compound, and ends at Santa Elena Canyon with 1,500 limestone cliffs rising above the Rio Grande.

You can get out and stretch your legs at a short trail that leads into the canyon. Now, you have two options: return by the same route or take the gravel Old Maverick Road to the western entrance of the park. Old Maverick Road is often passable by most vehicles, but may be impassable in heavy rains. A visitor center can give you information on current conditions.

Panther Junction to Rio Grande Village - 21 miles

This scenic drive goes past ancient limestone and offers many vistas across the river into Sierra del Carmen. The entire road drops about 2,000 feet in 20 miles. Stop at Dugout Wells and take a natural desert trail, find a great place to do some birdwatching, and have a picnic. Many also choose to soak in the Historic Hot Springs.

Stop for the short hike into Boquillas Canyon for one of the most picturesque spots in the area. Lastly, the Rio Grande Village Nature Trail offers a great spot to photograph or draw all sorts of local bird species.

Persimmon Gap to Panther Junction - 28 miles

This road runs between the north entrance of the park to Panther Junction. From Persimmon Gap the road descends into Tornillo Creek and Tornillo Flat. To the west, you'll see the Rosillos Mountains and the Dead Horse Mountains to the east. Worthwhile stops on this drive include the trails to Dog Canyon and Devil's Den, the Fossil Bone Exhibit, and the Tornillo Creek hoodoos.

Maverick Entrance Station to Panther Junction - 23 miles

This drive takes you through the desert scene and offers beautiful overlooks of the nearby mountains. There are several roadside exhibits that describe local wildlife you might encounter on the drive. Along with this route, you'll also find the junctions for the Chisos Basin road and the Ross Maxwell Scenic Drive.

IMPROVED DIRT SCENIC DRIVES

If you want to see a more primitive aspect of the park consider taking one of the improved dirt scenic drives. Most vehicles can access these roads, but some road conditions can be rough and deteriorate quickly with storms. Be sure to ask about the route in general before heading out on your drive.

Dagger Flat Auto Trail - seven miles

This road heads to the east and onto a small valley with a forest of giant dagger yuccas. In addition to vehicles, another great option would be crossing it on a mountain bike. The speed limit is 25 mph, and the road is narrow. Allow at least two hours for the entire round-trip drive. Seasonally, there may be sandy and muddy conditions; rain will also make the road difficult or impassable. Ask about road and weather conditions before heading out on your drive.

Grapevine Hills Road - 6.4 miles

After driving 6.4 miles down this road, you'll access Grapevine Hills trailhead. This trail is a 2.2-mile long round-trip toward the beautiful Balanced Rock. This road starts 3.3 miles west of Panther Junction and is generally passable by all vehicles. Past the trailhead, the road will require high-clearance vehicles, especially if there is any rain.

Hot Springs Road - two miles

The road is a rough, narrow wash that takes you to the Hot Springs Historic District. Nearby you'll be able to explore the ruins of J.O. Langford's resort. From the trailhead, you can hike to the hot springs in a half-mile round-trip hike. This is also a one-mile loop trail from the hot springs to the bluff above. A third trail will go toward to Daniels' Ranch in the Rio Grande Village about three miles to the east.

Old Maverick Road - 14 miles

It connects Maverick Junction and Santa Elena Canyon and takes you along Terlingua Creek and the badlands on the west side of the park. Near the road, you'll be able to visit numerous historic sites. This actual pathway is passable for most vehicles, but it is rough and washboarded. It will take you about an hour to drive the 14 miles. During rainy weather, this road is subject to high water and flooding.

PRIMITIVE DIRT SCENIC ROADS

There are also several miles of primitive and washboard dirt roads in the park that will take you through canyons and pass old settlements and cemeteries. You can use these roads to access hiking trails, primitive campsites, and the river. They are maintained for high-clearance vehicles only and may require a four-wheel drive at times due to the occasionally rugged terrain.

Check road conditions before heading out and come prepared; pack plenty of water, a jack, and a spare tire just in case (as well as someone who knows how to change a tire if you are unfamiliar with the practice).

Glenn Springs Road - 16 Miles

Leads you along the eastern side of the Chisos Mountains, then traverses the southwest corner of Chilicotal Mountain into Glenn Springs, a small desert spring. At one time in 1914, there was a large candelilla wax camp at this location. Today, this road requires four-wheel drive; from Glenn Springs to River Road, the road tends to become a little smoother.

Pine Canyon Road – 4 miles

From Glenn Springs Road you can take this short road that gradually climbs into Pine Canyon and gives you access to the Pine Canyon Trail.

Juniper Canyon Road – 5 miles

This is another short road from Glenn Springs Road that takes you to the Juniper Canyon Trail and the junction for Dodson Trail. This road is rocky and often requires a four-wheel drive.

Old Ore Road - 26 miles

This road was used in the early 1900s to transport ore from the mines in Mexico to the railroad at Marathon. It goes along the route that was once used by mule and pack trains. The road is rough and will require a sturdy vehicle. From here you can get a good look of the Chisos Mountains across Tornillo Creek to the west. At the southern end of the road, you'll reach a popular destination at Ernst Tinaja.

River Road - 51 miles

This road covers the southern part of the park and basically connects Rio Grande Village and Castolon. It typically follows the Rio Grande but is far enough away that you won't be able to see the river unless you take a side trip to a primitive site.

Due to the length of the road and the rough conditions, you should expect this drive to take a full day. Along the road you'll find primitive roadside campsites that will require a permit. The western end of the road is the roughest, so it can be best to backtrack from Mariscal Mine and exit through Glenn Springs Road.

Black Gap Road - 8.5 miles

This is a challenging road to drive that connects Glenn Springs Road with River Road. This road is not maintained and will require a four-wheel vehicle at all times.

After you've done some driving around and got a feel for the various areas of the park, you can choose where you want to focus your exploration. Big Bend National Park is a paradise for hikers and has one of the largest expanses of the road less public land in all of Texas.

There are over 150 miles of trail to choose from whether you are planning a day hike or a multi-night backpacking trip. Let's look at some of the hikes you can take.

DESERT HIKES

Desert trails in this park can be short and easy to multi-day hikes that are marked with rock cairns. Consider remote routes if you want a wilderness adventure, but these are only recommended for experienced hikers. The following are options for desert hikes:

Chihuahuan Desert Nature Trail - 0.5-mile round-trip – Easy

Starts at Dugout Wells, six miles southeast of Panther Junction.
This trail offers remnants of human settlements as well as the typical Chihuahuan Desert.

Chimneys Trail - 4.8-mile round-trip – Moderate

Starts at mile 13 of Ross Maxwell Scenic Drive.
Views of prominent volcanic dike formations.

Devil's Den - 5.6-mile round-trip – Moderate

Starts at the pull-off 3.5 miles south of the Persimmon Gap Visitor Center.
Travels through a limestone slot canyon.

Grapevine Hills Trail - 2.2-mile round-trip – Easy

Starts six miles down Grapevine Hills improved dirt road at a parking area.
Travels to a group of balanced rocks and an exposed laccolith.

Lower Burro Mesa Pouroff Trail - one-mile round-trip – Easy

Starts at the end of Burro Mesa Spur Road off Ross Maxwell Scenic Drive.
Travels through a gravel drainage and ends at box canyon with a 100-foot dropoff.

Marufo Vega - 1.2-mile round-trip – Strenuous

Starts at the Marufo Vega trailhead near Boquillas Canyon.
Pass through dry washes before dropping into Boquillas Canyon.

Mule Ears Spring Trail - 3.8-mile round-trip – Moderate

Starts at Mule Ears Overlook parking area at mile 15 of Ross Maxwell Scenic Drive.
Travels through the foothills of the Chisos Mountains and crosses several arroyos.

Panther Path - 50-yard loop – Easy

Starts at Panther Junction Visitor Center.
Wheelchair-accessible loop through a desert garden.
Sam Nail Ranch - 0.5-mile loop – Easy

Starts at mile three of Ross Maxwell Scenic Drive.
Well maintained trail that travels through the Nail Homestead.

Tuff Canyon - 0.75-mile round-trip – Easy

Starts at Tuff Canyon Overlook along the Ross Maxwell Scenic Drive.
Travels down into the canyon.

Upper Burro Mesa Pouroff Trail - 3.8-mile round-trip – Moderate

Starts at the pull-off at mile 6.6 of Ross Maxwell Scenic Drive.
Follows a dry wash to the top of a 100-foot pouroff.

MOUNTAIN HIKES

The Chisos Mountains rise to 7,832 feet and are filled with oaks, pines, junipers, madrones, and cypress. Within the mountains, there are about 20 miles of trails with excellent hiking opportunities. These trails are popular in the summer months when the mountains are cooler than the desert climates.

Boot Canyon Trail - 3.5 miles from trailhead then 2.8 miles to the South Rim – Strenuous

Starts at the Chisos Basin Trailhead.
Travels through the Chisos Mountains.

Chisos Basin Loop Trail - 1.8-mile round-trip – Moderate
Starts at the Chisos Basin Trailhead.
Travel in a counterclockwise direction for the easiest path.

Emory Peak - 10.5-mile round-trip – Strenuous

Starts at the Chisos Basin Trailhead.
Travels to the peak of the highest point in the park.

Lost Mine Trail - 4.8-mile round-trip – Moderate

Starts at mile 5.1 on Basin Road.
Travels through the forest and ends at the ridgeline.

South Rim - 12 to 14.5-mile round-trip – Strenuous

Starts at the Basin Trailhead.
The trail climbs 2,000 feet to the South Rim.

Window Trail - 5.6-mile round-trip – Moderate

Starts at the Chisos Basin Trailhead.

Drops through Oak Creek Canyon to the Window pouroff and the desert.

Window View Trail - 0.3-mile round-trip – Easy

Starts at the Chisos Basin Trailhead.
The wheelchair-accessible trail that circles a low hill with views of the mountains.

River Hikes

Much of the river that runs through the park is fronted by stands of reeds and mesquite. This makes the river difficult to access, but a great place to observe wildlife. There are a few short hikes that provide access to the river.

Boquillas Canyon Trail - 1.4-miles round-trip – Moderate

Starts at the end of the Boquillas Canyon Spur Road.
Climbs to a cliff overlooking the river then continues down to the river's edge.

Hot Springs Canyon Trail - six-mile round-trip – Moderate

Starts at Daniel's Ranch or Hot Springs.
Runs close to the river in specific places and travels the rim of Hot Springs Canyon.

Hot Springs Historic Trail - one-mile round-trip – Easy

Starts at the Hot Springs parking lot.
Travels by the remains of a resort, homestead, and hot springs.

Rio Grande Village Nature Trail - 0.75-mile loop – Easy

Starts at Rio Grande Village Campground, Site #18.

Excellent trail for wildlife-viewing gradually climbs a hill.

Santa Elena Canyon Trail - 1.7-mile round-trip – Moderate

Starts at the terminus of Ross Maxwell Scenic Drive.

The trail travels into Santa Elena Canyon, impassable when the creek floods.

ITINERARY #2: SOUTH DAKOTA

BADLANDS AND WIND CAVE

These two parks can combine for a nice two-week trip. Badlands is a great place to discover more about flora and fauna through one of the numerous hiking trails. In Wind Cave, there are several tours to do below ground while there are plenty of hiking trails to explore above ground as well. Let's look at what both of these parks have to offer so you can plan an itinerary and see how long you need to spend at each park.

BADLANDS

There are plenty of activities at Badlands, from camping and hiking to bird-watching and auto touring. There is no shortage of little too epic escapades at Badlands National Park. Perhaps the biggest activity to do consists of hiking and there are a variety of hiking trails that you can use to explore the park up close.

Stop by the visitor center to get information on the trail and which ones are best for your fitness and experience level. If you want to get into the wilderness, then consider a backpacking experience.

Before you head out on your hike there are a few things you need to remember:

1. Always carry at least two quarts of water per person per two-hour hike.
2. It is best to wear a hat and sunglasses.
3. You should pack rain gear since weather conditions change rapidly.
4. Wear sturdy boots to protect your feet from cactus spines and blisters.

5. Remember to stay at least 100 yards away from all the wildlife you encounter. If wildlife reacts to you, then you are too close.
6. All park resources are to remain as you've found them.

HIKING TRAILS

Door Trail - 0.75-mile round-trip – Easy

Boardwalk trail that goes through a break in the Badlands Wall known as "the Door" so you can get a view of the Badlands.

Window Trail - 0.25-mile round-trip – Easy

The trail leads to a natural window in the Badlands Wall with a vast open sight of the canyon and its intricate erosions.

Notch Trail - 1.5-miles round-trip - Moderate to Strenuous

This trail travels through a canyon, then climbs a log ladder and follows a ledge to "the Notch" to display the White River Valley. Do not attempt to complete it in rainy weather.

Castle Trail - 10-mile round-trip – Moderate

This is the longest trail in the park and starts at the Door and Window parking area. A mostly leveled trail that passes most of the badlands formations.

Cliff Shelf - 0.5-mile round-trip – Moderate

This loop trail is a boardwalk with some stairs to climb. A good trail for wildlife observation.

Saddle Pass - 0.25-mile round-trip – Strenuous

This short trail climbs the Badlands Wall to face the White River Valley.

Medicine Root Loop - four miles – Moderate

This rolling trail allows you to explore the mixed-grass prairie while providing distance views of the Badlands.

Fossil Exhibit Trail - 0.25-mile round-trip – Easy

A boardwalk trail that has fossil replicas and exhibits of creatures that once lived in the area.

WIND CAVE

Once you've finished hiking all parts of Badlands National Park, you can head to the second part of your two-week trip at Wind Cave. Here you'll want to spend time both above and below ground. Whichever you want to start with is fine– you can mix them up and do both in a day. Let's look at your options.

CAVE TOURS

There are three regular walking tours you can take:

GARDEN OF EDEN TOUR – EASY

- Enters and exits by elevator.
- Lasts one hour.
- Covers ⅓ of a mile and feature 150 stairs.
- Sticks mostly to the upper level of the cave with common formations.

NATURAL ENTRANCE TOUR – MODERATE

- Enters near the natural entrance and exits by elevator.
- Last about an hour and a half.
- Covers ⅔ miles and includes 300 stairs, mostly going down.
- Goes to the middle of the cave with abundant boxwork formations.

FAIRGROUNDS TOUR – STRENUOUS

- Enters and exits by the elevator.
- Lasts an hour and a half.
- Cover ⅔ of a mile and includes 450 stairs.
- Covers both upper and middle levels of the cave.

In addition, there are two specialty tours you can take of the cave if you are more adventurous.

The Candlelight Tour is strenuous and includes some traveling off trail. Only those older than eight years old are allowed. You will experience the cave by candlelight just as early explorers did. The tour occurs in the less developed and unlighted portion of the cave. You will be given a candle bucket to carry. The tour is limited to 10 people and is only available in summer months.

The Wild Cave Tour is very strenuous and requires some crawling. The minimum age for this tour is 16, and that is with signed parent permission. It lasts hours and introduces you to basic safe caving. It is best to wear old clothes and gloves since you'll be crawling. Hard hats, lights, and kneepads are provided by the park. The tour is limited to 10 people.

Once you are finished exploring underground, take the time to explore all this park has to offer above ground.

HIKING TRAILS

Wind Cave National Park features over 30 miles of hiking trails through a mixed-grass prairie and ponderosa pine forest. Before heading out on a hike make sure you are prepared:

- Carry and drink plenty of water while hiking.
- Before taking a hike check the weather and bring extra layers if needed.
- Large wildlife is present in the park so be aware of your surroundings at all times. You are required to stay at least 25 yards away from bison and elk.
- Off-trail hiking is allowed, but make sure you have a topographical map of the area.

Easy Trails

Elk Mountain - 1.2 miles
Loops around the Elk Mountain Campground

Prairie Vista - one mile
Starts at the visitor center or picnic area north of the visitor center
Rankin Ridge - one mile
Takes you to the highest point in the park

Wind Cave Canyon - 1.8 miles
A good hike for birdwatching

Moderate Trails

Cold Brook Canyon - 1.4 miles
Takes you down into the canyon and crosses a prairie dog town.

Lookout Point - 2.2 miles

Follows the rolling hills and then descends to Beaver Creek.

STRENUOUS TRAILS

Sanctuary - 3.6 miles

Follows the prairie and passes a large prairie dog town and several former homesteads.

East Bison Flats - 3.7 miles

Provides panoramas of the prairie, Buffalo Gap, and the Black Hills.

Centennial - six miles

Crosses prairies, ponderosa forests and follows Beaver Creek.

Highland Creek - 8.6 miles

The most diverse and longest trail in the park.

Boland Ridge - 2.6 miles

Climbs up from the Red Valley off Road NPS 6, popular trail for viewing elk.

ITINERARY #3: FLORIDA

EVERGLADES, DRY TORTUGAS, AND BISCAYNE

Florida offers excellent beaches and plenty of nature to explore. Spend two weeks traveling among Everglades, Dry Tortugas, and Biscayne to immerse yourself in all the types of nature Florida has to offer.

Spend a few days checking out the few hiking trails and guided tours of the Everglades. Then experience a backcountry campout on the islands of Dry Tortugas for a few nights. Finish your stay with a fulfilling hike and laying on sun-baked soft sand with the splash of waves at your feet.

EVERGLADES

Everglades National Park is the third largest park in the lower 48 states at over 2,400 miles. There are plenty of outdoor activities to enjoy at this park, including hiking and water-related endeavors. Let's consider all you can do at this park so you can start planning your itinerary and seeing how many days you need to spend here.

BICYCLING

The best bicycling happens at Shark Valley, the Snake Bight Trail near Flamingo, and along the Long Pine Key Nature Trail.

BIRDWATCHING

Whether it is the great blue heron or a flock of spoonbills, there are plenty of bird species to see at the Everglades, and birdwatching is sure to be a rewarding experience.

Boating

Since most of the Everglades is only accessible by boat, it is a popular way to experience the park. Whether you arrive on your own boat, rent one or take a tour, boating will get your closer to the wilderness of the park.

Camping

Everglades National Park offers both front country and backcountry camping depending on how much of a wilderness experience you want. Long Pine Key and Flamingo campgrounds have drinking water, picnic tables, grills, restrooms, and both tent or trailer sites. Flamingo does have some showers and electric hookups. In the watery backcountry of the park, you can find some primitive campsites and beach sites.

Kayaking and Canoeing

This is perhaps the best way to experience the wildlife and vegetation of the Everglades. The Wilderness Waterway is 99 miles and would take you seven to 10 days to explore, but there are many smaller trails you can take.

Fishing

Everglades is a popular spot for both freshwater and saltwater sports fishing. You can charter boats out of Flamingo. Be sure to check the visitor center for regulations pertaining to the types of fish you can catch, how many of them, and any areas that are closed to fishing.

Hiking

The Everglades offers short interpretative trails as well as longer hikes.

Pine Island Short Interpretive Trails:

- ☐ Anhinga Trail
- ☐ Gumbo Limbo Trail
- ☐ Pinelands Trail
- ☐ Pahayokee Overlook
- ☐ Mahogany Hammock Trail

Flamingo Short Interpretive Trails:

- ☐ West Lake Trail
- ☐ Snake Bight Trail
- ☐ Rowdy Bend Trail
- ☐ Christian Point Trail
- ☐ Bear Lake Trail
- ☐ Eco Pond Trail
- ☐ Guy Bradley Trail
- ☐ Bayshore Trail
- ☐ Coastal Prairie Trail

Flamingo Canoe Trails:

- ☐ Hells Bay Canoe Trail
- ☐ Nine Mile Pond Canoe Trail

Shark Valley Short Interpretive Trails:
- ☐ Otter Cave Hammock
- ☐ Bobcat Boardwalk

RANGER GUIDED PROGRAMS

Perhaps one of the best ways to learn about the park and the area is to take a ranger-guided activity. These include hikes, canoe trips, slough slogs, bicycle trips, tram tours, and campfire programs. Check with the visitor center to see what the days and times are for current programs.

Slough Slogging

If you want to experience some off-trail hiking and don't mind getting your feet wet then check out this unique option. You will get up close and personal with the watery parts of the park. Make sure you pack up an extra pair of clothes with you after treading through the water and reeds.

Tours

In addition to ranger-guided activities, there are other guided tours you can take through the park. Concession boat captains offer boat tours along the mangrove coast of Flamingo and Gulf Coast. Tram Tour naturalists take you through the Shark River Slough.

Wildlife Viewing

There is a cornucopia of wild creatures to behold and marvel at while visiting this park. From scaly alligators to multi-colored screeching birds and fish, you're sure to encounter wildlife at some point.

Dry Tortugas

The best way to experience Dry Tortugas National Park is by spending a night or two at one of the primitive sites on one of the small islands. This is a great place to get away from it all and truly dive into aquatic adventures.

Most of this park is open water, but there are seven small islands in addition to the Fort Jefferson tours that the park is known for. Head out to some of the islands for the following activities.

Garden Key

This is the second largest island in the park and is about 14 acres in size. This island features the popular Fort Jefferson as well as the visitor center, campgrounds, and an array of water activities. The following activities are available on this island:

- Boating
- Camping
- Fishing
- Snorkeling
- Swimming
- Wildlife-Viewing
- Night Sky Viewing
- Ranger-Led Activities
- Paddlesports

Loggerhead Key

This is the largest island in the park and is the site of many shipwrecks, a lighthouse, and the historic Carnegie Laboratory for Marine Ecology.

This island is named for the number of loggerhead sea turtles that are found in the water and is accessible only through a private vessel. All visitors need to stay on marked day paths and are not permitted to spend the night. The following activities are available:

- Boating

- Hiking
- Wildlife-Viewing
- Swimming
- Snorkeling
- Paddlesports

Bush Key

This undeveloped and subtropical island is best explored in late fall and early winter, during breeding season for many birds that can't be seen anywhere else in the United States. The island is only 16 acres in size and is open to visitors only after the nesting wildlife are gone.

Bush Key has a one-mile round-trip trail that takes you around the shoreline, which is always worthwhile a visit. At times this section of the park is accessible by a land bridge from Garden Key, and at other times you can only access it by kayak or canoe.

Biscayne

Just outside of the bustling city of Miami, Biscayne offers a break and a chance to enjoy nature. As with other National Parks in Florida, Biscayne is a popular destination for water activities. Let's consider some of the outdoor activities you can do– most of which are on the water since the park only has one mile of paved roadway.

Fishing

Because of the unique marine habitat preserved and the nursery environment here, there are world-class opportunities for fishing when it comes to spiny lobster, snapper, grouper, tarpon, and bonefish.

Guided Tours

At the Dante Fascell Visitor Center, you can check the schedule for guided boat tours. This allows you to relax and enjoy the scenery while learning about the history, wildlife, and ecosystems found within.

Kayaking and Canoeing

This is the best way to explore the shallow bay waters as well as the mangrove-lined shorelines.

Diving and Snorkeling

Along the Maritime Heritage Trail, you'll find some excellent opportunities for diving and snorkeling. You can even explore the remains of some shipwrecks.

Boating

With 95 percent of the park being water, boating is the best way to explore the protected waters of the bay as well as the northernmost Florida Keys.

Wildlife Watching

Biscayne is home to over 500 species of reef fish along with an estimated 20 threatened and endangered species within the park boundaries. This makes wildlife-viewing an excellent opportunity both in and out of the water. Do respect these animals and understand you are in their habitat.

Avoid feeding them anything falling under the category of 'human food,' NEVER litter, call a park ranger if you see something out of place, and always keep a safe distance from their marked territories.

LAST WORD

These are only a few of the many national parks scattered all throughout the United States, but they are incredibly worthwhile. They are natural landmarks for a reason, after all; it is not every day that one can find the largest living tree on Earth or a waterfall that looks as though it is flowing with liquid flaming gold. There is so much to see in this world, and these locations remind us of our insignificance compared to the powerful ground below us.

The earthy scent of falling rain, the crackle of gravel beneath our feet, the sensation of sunlight coating your skin. You cannot find that within the screen of a laptop or a phone.

Every now and then, it is a fundamental part of life to press a pause button on the world with day-to-day commodities and technology, and simply become one with nature, as we were once so many years ago. Being able to look top of a mountain at the world below you after hours of sweat and a burning feeling in your muscles during that last strenuous mile is one of the best, most unforgettable moments you will ever experience.

If hiking is not that much of a hobby or a way of life for you, simply taking a walk or photographing what you see in order to capture a single second of the sheer world of wonders in front of you is also more than enough.

Hopefully, this guide allowed you to brainstorm plans and future long-term trips to either of these national parks with friends, family, or even by your own accord as you search once again for the ultimate human connection to the planet we live in. Thank you, and best of luck in your adventures.

If you are interested in reading and learning about the all the National Parks in the Eastern United States, looks for my third and final book in this series.

Lastly, I want to say THANK YOU for purchasing and reading my book. I really hope you got a lot out of it!

Can I ask you for a quick favor though?

If you enjoyed this book, I would really appreciate it if you could leave me a Review.

I LOVE getting feedback from my wonderful readers, and reviews really do make the difference. I read all of my reviews and would love to hear your thoughts.

I also want to ask for your help and forgiveness ahead of time, in the event if you find any errors, typos or outdated information, please feel free to email me so I can fix the mistake.

bushcrafttrainer@gmail.com

Last but not the least, I want to extend my heartfelt thanks to the following organizations for some of the amazing images we shared in this guide.

http://commons.wikimedia.org

flickr.com

nps.gov

lib.utexas.edu

scoutingmagazine.org

npmaps.com

forum.skyscraperpage.com

segd.org

hikeourplanet.com

pr.com

irvoslin.wordpress.com

mapquest.com

swmaps.com

Thank you so much!!

Rob J. Simms

A FINAL NOTE

The crucial bond between human and nature solidifies as we tread among the many wonders of a world untouched by the intangible grasp of screens and Tweets. There is nothing, absolutely nothing, similar to the feeling of washing your face in a fresh cold stream of clean mountain water after a long adventure in the presence of chirping birds and quiet deer.

Nothing like standing on top of a cliff with wind-packed with the cleanest air you will ever breathe as you overlook a burning magenta sunset giving way to the stars.

The outdoors we find in these natural parks are the true land of milk and honey, with a sweetness reaching the tip of your tongue and the depths of your heart.

Step out of the daily concerns of work and money and dare to venture into the world we have always belonged to, but have forgotten throughout the years.

Made in the USA
Columbia, SC
10 April 2019